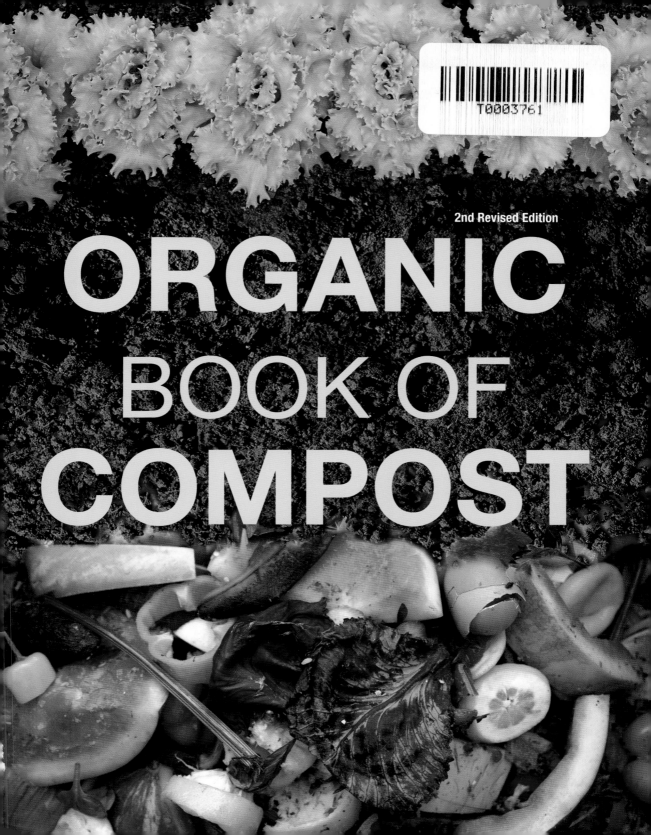

2nd Revised Edition

ORGANIC BOOK OF COMPOST

Published 2020—IMM Lifestyle Books
www.IMMLifestyleBooks.com

IMM Lifestyle Books are distributed in the UK by
Grantham Book Service, Trent Road, Grantham,
Lincolnshire, NG31 7XQ.

In North America, IMM Lifestyle Books are distributed by
Fox Chapel Publishing, 903 Square Street, Mount Joy, PA
17552, *www.FoxChapelPublishing.com*.

ISBN 978-1-5048-0123-2

The Cataloging-in-Publication Data is on file with the
Library of Congress.

We are always looking for talented authors. To submit an
idea, please send a brief inquiry to
acquisitions@foxchapelpublishing.com.

Printed in Singapore
10 9 8 7 6 5 4 3

2nd Revised Edition

ORGANIC
BOOK OF
COMPOST

Easy and Natural Techniques to Feed Your Garden

PAULINE PEARS

IMM **lifestyle** ::**books**™

Read. Learn. Do What You Love.

CONTENTS

INTRODUCTION

Composting makes the world go round. It recycles the nutrients that make plants (and animals) grow, feeds the bugs that keep the soil healthy and is a sustainable, low-cost way of dealing with "rubbish that rots." And it can be fun too.

Looking at a handful of compost you might wonder what all the fuss is about. How could a whole book be written about something that looks like "dirt." How can people be so passionate about a process that goes on in the natural world all the time? We hope that by the time you have made your first batch of compost you will be equally inspired – or at the very least feel that it is something worth doing again.

WHAT IS GARDEN COMPOST?

It is important to be clear about what is meant by the word "compost." Compost, which looks like a rich dark-brown soil, is a product that results from the slow decomposition of plant and animal matter by living organisms. It is nature's way of recycling the nutrients that exist in all living plants and animals and returning them to the soil to enrich and feed further generations of flora and fauna.

Compost is not the same as the seed, potting and multi-purpose composts on sale in garden shops. These, which are more correctly called growing media, are carefully formulated mixtures, designed for the specific purpose of raising and growing plants.

Compost-making is for everyone. You don't need to be a keen gardener or have a science

degree – the advice and instructions in this book are given in clear and simple terms.

A METHOD FOR EVERY SITUATION

Compost can be made in back yards, small or large gardens, school playgrounds, and on balconies and boats. This book has methods to suit every situation – including cool heaps, worm composting, Bokashi treatment and compost tumblers. There are also techniques to fit a range of lifestyles. Some composting methods involve little time and effort, while others can be turned into an enjoyable hobby. Choose the one that suits you and your family best; composting can be a great activity for children too. If you are new to composting, this book will show you how to get started, using a method that suits the range of items that you have available to compost. Within the chapter entitled "Getting Started" there is a flow chart to help you choose the method that suits your circumstances (see pages 36–37). If you

Right Composting need not involve much work. Heap suitable materials into a compost bin and let nature do the rest.

have already tried making compost and are not satisfied with the results, this book will help you to work out what you need to do to achieve your aims.

There is a chapter on composting containers and where to put them, a chapter devoted to worm composting, and one on other techniques and treatments with full instructions on how to proceed. There is also a chapter focused on the helpful creatures that live in your compost and how they do their work.

"Can I compost it?" is a frequently asked question. At the heart of this book is an invaluable chart to refer to when you are unsure if a particular item is suitable for composting. This list might also encourage you to compost and recycle items that you might not have thought of before (see "What can I compost" pages 64–77).

Making compost, leaf mold and so on should not be an end in itself. The recycling process is only really complete when the product is put back on to the soil (or into your pots and containers), and the plant foods it contains are used again by growing plants. This book also includes advice on how to make best use of the products you have made.

Above A handful of worm compost will pep up a hanging basket.

Left Compost is such wonderful stuff that it is often referred to as "black gold."

GARDEN ORGANIC

This book has been written by a team of experts at Garden Organic, the UK's charity for organic gardening. The organization, founded as the Henry Doubleday Research Association (HDRA) by Lawrence D. Hills, has been promoting organic gardening in homes, communities and schools since the 1950s.

Compost-making is at the heart of organic gardening, where the aim is to minimize the need to use outside resources and materials, and reduce the risk of polluting the wider environment. Developing biodiversity in the garden is also a key feature of organic gardening. Treating the soil with compost helps to increase biodiversity in the soil, which helps to maintain soil health. It has even been shown to help plants resist some pests and diseases. No surprise then that Garden Organic has been promoting composting for over 60 years. The charity works with individuals, communities, schools and care providers, helping them with practical advice on how to develop gardening projects and grow organically. We also house the Heritage Seed Library. This collection conserves rare vegetable varieties that are no longer commercially available. To support the charity or become a member visit www.gardenorganic.org.uk.

Garden Organic has been a major player in the modernization of home composting. Its work – giving advice and training advisors – has helped thousands of people make compost successfully. Garden Organic also established the Composting Association for large and industrial-scale composting. Now an independent organization, the Organics Recycling Group works with the huge industry that composting has become.

Left The biodynamic garden at Ryton Gardens.

Right The Cook's Garden at Ryton Gardens grows an amazing array of decorative and edible plants.

An overview of Ryton Gardens – demonstration organic gardens in Warwickshire.

1 COMPOSTING THEN AND NOW

People have been making compost, in some form or another, for thousands of years. But in fact what they have really been doing is simply replicating, in a rather more organized form, what nature has been doing for a great deal longer. You only have to "kick" your way across a woodland floor to see the quality of nature's compost! So, composting is a process that is as old as time, but it is also totally up-to-date, ticking all the boxes for a sustainable, twenty-first century lifestyle.

Above and right Every part of the garden will benefit from the addition of compost.

COMPOSTING FOR GROWING

A plant takes up minerals from the soil as it grows. When it dies it decays and is taken back into the soil by worms and other creatures. The same happens to animals. This is how nature recycles nutrients, so the land continues to be productive. Until the advent of "artificial," man-made fertilizers around 60 years ago, this was also the way gardeners and farmers kept their land fertile. Then the majority abandoned recycling and compost-making in favour of the "granules from the bag." Of course, the plant and animal wastes that had once been recycled in farms and gardens had to be disposed of somehow. Burning and dumping waste in landfill sites were two popular options – both with environmental drawbacks.

This became the common practice, apart from those committed to organic farming and gardening. Lawrence D. Hills, founder of Garden Organic, was one of those who were not convinced that the "chemical" road was the one to follow for long-term sustainability. In the twenty-first century, his fears appear to have been well founded.

COMPOST AS WASTE DISPOSAL

In the 1990s a number of apparently disparate issues came together – and the result was compost! Environmentalists called for strategies for waste minimization and recycling, proposing a target of 25 percent for household waste recycling by the year 2000. Local authorities realized that recycling bottles, paper and other items alone could not meet this target. They began to consider how to deal with the "putrescible" fraction of the waste (items such as kitchen and garden waste that can rot and smell), which made up around 30–40 percent of the contents of the average garbage can at that time. One relatively low-cost partial solution to the problem was home composting. Since then composting has become a recognized method of waste disposal.

At that time Garden Organic was one of the main sources of practical advice on home composting. It set up a local authority membership scheme to deal with the flood of enquiries. Other organizations helped localities minimize waste and make best use of resources. Home composting programs enabled local authorities to encourage home composting, in particular offering low-cost compost bins to householders.

EDUCATION AND SUPPORT

It became clear that more education and support was needed if the local residents were to compost effectively. It was to help address this issue that Garden Organic started its Master Composter scheme – based on the US model. Garden Organic's Master Composters are volunteers who spend time promoting home composting in their local community, encouraging householders to take up composting and ensuring those already composting continue to do so effectively. Master Composters come from many backgrounds and age groups; their unifying feature is their enthusiasm for encouraging more environmentally friendly waste management practices. Volunteers, after the necessary training, work in their community to promote composting and to give help and advice to individuals, communities and schools.

Left Worms will work their way through a huge variety of compostable waste, turning it into a valuable resource.

FROM PIGS TO WORMS

The lifestyle and living conditions of the new generations being encouraged to make compost meant that composting methods needed an update. The traditional advice – to make a large compost heap, carefully constructed over a short period of time, that heated up to steaming temperatures and was turned regularly – was no longer appropriate for the majority wanting to use composting
as a means of waste management. Fortunately, composting still works very well in smaller, neat-looking compost bins that are filled on an ad hoc basis and otherwise ignored.

The Centre for Alternative Technology took a fresh look at what could be composted from the waste items produced by modern households. This turned out to be kitchen waste and lots of low-grade cardboard and paper. This led to the development of the high-fiber heap using just these items. Adding egg boxes, cardboard cartons, and so on to a compost bin is now common practice. The move to vegetable-based printing inks removed the concern over contamination from cadmium and other heavy metals traditionally used in printing.

In the past, many households would have kept a pig in the back yard to convert food scraps into manure and useful meat. The modern equivalent, but without the smell, is worm composting. Worms for fishing bait are raised on compostable waste. As you don't need a garden to make worm compost, it extends the scope of composting considerably.

DANGERS?

There were rumors that home composting, that most innocuous of pastimes, might have its dangers. This came out of the 2001 foot-and-mouth epidemic in the UK, which cost the country millions. It relates to the composting of food waste from domestic kitchens. The fear was that unless the disposal of this waste was strictly controlled, foot-and-mouth disease would continue to spread.

Fortunately, home composting is still quite legal and generally safe. It is fine to make compost on the premises where it originates, and to use the compost on the land at those premises, as long as pigs or ruminants (cattle, goats and sheep) are not kept there. If there is poultry on the premises, composting may be done, but it must be done in a closed container.

FULL CIRCLE

The recent revival of interest in growing
fruit and vegetables at home and in
allotments, now with many more people
using organic methods, takes us full circle.
Homemade compost is just what the garden
needs to grow healthy, productive crops, in
a sustainable way.

Above Growing your own fruit and vegetables is made
easier and more sustainable if you make your own
valuable compost.

2 WHY COMPOST?

Composting is something that humankind has been doing for centuries, but in this day and age, why should we as individuals bother? We now know that typically over 40 percent of household waste can be composted, but why not leave it for local authorities to deal with? Does home composting really solve any problems? Can something as simple as composting kitchen and garden waste help mitigate the effects of climate change? Can it benefit you or your children? If you are not interested in gardening or only have a balcony or tiny backyard, is it worth the trouble? The answer to all those questions is "yes." Read on to find out the many reasons why home composting is a worthwhile and beneficial practice.

BENEFITS TO YOU

Turning waste into something of value, rather than just passing it on to someone else to deal with, is very empowering. Taking responsibility means that you are reducing the impact of the waste you produce on the wider community and environment.

These days there are so many large environmental issues such as climate change that seem too big for an individual to do anything about, but composting is something that we can all do. Composting can help the average household cut the amount of waste it puts in the bin (or recycling box) by 40 percent – a considerable figure. The small task of starting to home compost means that you will be helping to work towards a sustainable future.

ORGANIC GARDENING

If you have a garden and aim to manage it organically, then making compost is essential. Home composting plays a key role in organic growing – compost helps keep plants healthy and can make it easier to avoid the use of pesticides.

SAVING MONEY AND TIME

Making compost, leaf mold and mulches reduces the amount of money you spend on buying fertilizers, soil conditioner and potting composts. Using these home-produced products reduces the need for

watering – a valuable time-saver and cost-cutter if your water is on a meter.

Millions of tons of food are thrown away every year after purchase – this is good food that doesn't actually get to the table but is thrown away before being prepared or eaten. Collecting food waste to compost helps to make you aware of how much food your household is wasting and may concentrate your mind when it comes to shopping. This

Below Adding homemade compost to your plants is environmentally responsible and reduces the need for water and fertilizer.

Above Collecting kitchen waste for composting can actually help reduce the quantity of food that you waste.

new awareness may not help your compost heap, but it could be good for your budget!

Reducing the volume of waste that your public works needs to collect and recycle may also help cut its costs, which can only be good for taxes. Reducing the amount of trash that we dispose of is not only desirable, it is becoming increasingly necessary as we run out of suitable landfill sites and require greater capacity to burn waste for energy.

SLIM YOUR BIN

Home composting can cut the speed at which your garbage can fills up, and reduce the risk of unpleasant odors from the bin. With cuts in the frequency of garbage collection in many areas, this can be an important issue.

SLIM YOURSELF

Composting could keep you fitter and healthier. A bit far fetched you may think? None of the jobs connected with making compost are particularly strenuous, however, every little bit adds up. Think of the daily stroll to and from the compost bin, turning the heap (if that's the method you decide upon), harvesting the finished compost and, finally, spreading it on the garden. In addition to this, being outside, either making or using your compost, will help give you the "feel-good factor."

ENGAGING CHILDREN

Children soon take to the idea of putting waste in a compost bin rather than into the garbage can. This helps to raise awareness of all sorts of other environmental issues vital to their future.

An amazing number of creatures live in a compost heap – from woodlice to toads, from beetles to worms. You can find more in on pages 156–167. This makes compost a fascinating resource for children (and adults) to explore.

BENEFITS TO THE GARDEN

Making compost turns vegetable scraps, cereal boxes, weeds, fruit peels, egg boxes and a host of other unlikely items into that high-quality soil improver and fertility builder, compost. Composting recycles all the plant foods in these "waste products" into a form that can be used again by the millions of tiny creatures that live in the soil, and by the plants growing in it.

Compost could be seen as a "wholefood" providing nutrients in a balanced form, and lots of fiber! When you add compost to your garden, the soil-living creatures get to work to break it down further, meanwhile improving the soil and making nutrients available to growing plants. The chapter entitled "How to use your compost" (see page 138) explains how compost and other recycled garden products can be used to enhance and improve your garden, whatever its style and size.

Below Homemade compost is all that these cabbages need to produce a good crop. The benefits to garden flowers are evident too.

How compost benefits the garden

- Makes your garden grow!

- Makes heavy clay soil lighter, so it drains better and is easier for plant roots to penetrate.

- Adds "body" to light soil so that it holds on to water and plant foods, thus reducing the need for feeding and watering.

- Feeds the millions of soil-living creatures that keep the soil healthy.

- Helps plants to resist pest and disease attack.

Left This crop of sweetcorn and beans has benefited from homemade compost. Herbs and flowers (above) will also show the results of compost use.

NO MORE BONFIRES!

Although bonfires are banned in many areas now, they can still be a common sight (and smell) in some places. This is a waste of resources and is unnecessary, particularly as nearly all weeds and crop wastes can be composted and broken down, returning their nutrients to the soil.

BENEFITS FOR THE FUTURE ENVIRONMENT

We are told that we must make lifestyle changes to reduce the impact of climate change and minimize our personal carbon footprint. How can home composting kitchen scraps and garden rubbish make a difference?

SAVING PEAT BOGS

Homemade compost, leaf mold and mulches can be used in the garden in place of peat and peat-based seed and potting composts used by amateur gardeners.

So why is using peat a problem?

Peat is the result of thousands of years of plants slowly decomposing in waterlogged, acidic conditions. We have been using this resource so quickly in recent times that there is no opportunity for it to replenish itself.

Like the tropical rainforests that so many people have fought to preserve, peat bogs provide the habitat for a huge diversity of plant and animal life, from mosses to birds. These areas should be preserved before they are destroyed forever. Peat extraction not only disturbs rare wildlife but also releases carbon dioxide (one of the main "greenhouse gases" responsible for global warming) into the atmosphere every year. Bogs contain millions of tons of carbon.

WILDLIFE HABITAT

The compost bin itself provides an extra habitat for wildlife in your garden. As well as the millions of microscopic and tiny creatures that do the composting, others, such as worms, lizards and snakes (increasing rarities) may find a compost bin an attractive place to live for a while.

REDUCE GREENHOUSE GASSES

When kitchen scraps and garden prunings (biodegradable waste) are buried in a landfill site they decay without oxygen, unlike composting which is an aerobic (with oxygen) process. This means that methane is produced, another gas that is a major contributor to the greenhouse effect, which causes global warming.

Landfill operators now have measures to capture methane, using it, for example, to power generators on site and also add energy back into the national grid. However, this equipment is costly to install and maintain, and there is still some loss of gas.

SUSTAINABLE AND LOCAL MEANS ENERGY EFFICIENT

Home composting is remarkably energy efficient in several respects. These days an increasing volume of the biodegradable waste collected by local authorities, and that delivered to recycling centers, will be composted. This is much better than putting it into landfill, but it still has an environmental impact in the amount of energy used to transport and process the waste. In some cases you can buy the resulting compost (which is better than using peat) but this is often packaged in plastic sacks and also needs to be transported, thus consuming valuable energy resources.

The only energy required for home composting is yours! Using home compost and other home-recycled products on the garden in place of purchased products will also save the energy required for their production, packaging and distribution. Fertilizers can be very energy-intensive to produce; some are based on dwindling natural resources and may be imported from distant countries.

CUT LANDFILL

Over the last few decades we have been filling up landfill sites (basically holes in the ground) with rubbish. This is not a sustainable option. Landfill sites can pollute the environment and suitable sites are becoming increasingly scarce.

One of the current alternatives to landfill is "Energy from Waste," which includes incineration. This is not a popular alternative with the general public because of the perceived issue of local environmental impact.

Both landfill and incineration are huge wastes of natural resources. The more that householders can reduce the volume of waste they throw away, the less will be the need for either landfill sites or for controversial incinerators.

CONCLUSIONS

Individuals make compost for all sorts of different reasons – from saving time and money to being able to show their children all the amazing creatures that live in a compost bin. Pick your own reasons and give it a go!

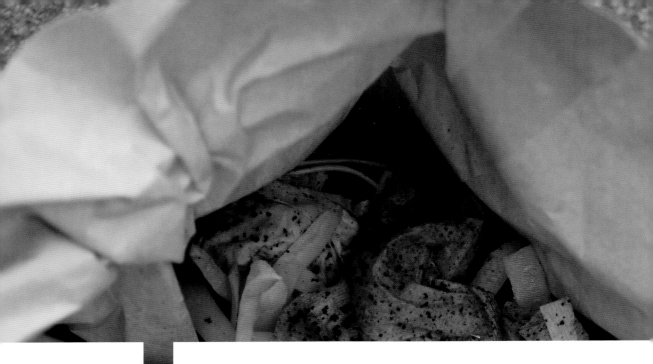

3 GETTING STARTED

So you've got lots of reasons to get composting, but where on earth do you start? This chapter looks at some of the things you need to consider to help you decide how to begin and what method to use. Where to put a container, what sorts of materials you might want to compost and which methods might be right for your circumstances are all addressed in the following pages.

WHERE TO START

There are a number of considerations to keep in mind when trying to determine which method of composting might be right for your circumstances. Where do you live and what do you want to recycle?

EQUIPMENT

Composting doesn't need any expensive high-tech equipment; as you will learn in the next chapter, the composting organisms do most of the work for you. The only equipment needed is a container for your compost. This could be a plastic compost bin purchased locally, a sophisticated compost tumbler or just a few old pallets nailed together quite roughly and placed somewhere in your garden.

LOCATION

You will also want to think about where to place your compost container. Generally it should be somewhere accessible that receives some direct sunlight. You also want to make it a convenient distance from your kitchen to encourage you to make frequent trips with your kitchen waste and paper. Look at the section entitled "A home for your compost," page 78, for more information and ideas on location. Keep in mind that you do not need a garden to start composting; it is perfectly possible to have a small compost box on a balcony or in a small backyard.

COMPOSTING MATERIALS

The next thing that you need is material to put in your compost container. In the section entitled "What can I compost?," page 60, we look what you can recycle and define these materials as either being "greens" or "browns." Greens are wet, sappy materials that break down quickly and browns are dry, fibrous materials that are slower to decompose. A good compost heap needs a balance of both kinds of materials. Too many greens and your compost heap will be too wet, too many browns and it will be too dry; both situations will result in your compost heap not working to its full capacity.

Another question asked by all those new to composting is "can I compost this item or not?"; again the section entitled "What can I compost?" will answer many of these questions.

Right Once you get started, you may find that you need more than one compost bin.

CHOOSING THE RIGHT METHOD FOR YOU

If you ask five people for advice on the "right" or "best" way to make compost, you are likely to get five different answers. There are many ways of making compost. The best one for you is the method that suits your lifestyle, the time you want to spend on composting, how quickly you want to produce compost, and, most importantly, what sorts of materials you have available from which to make your compost.

The flow chart on pages 36–37 aims to help you make these decisions, starting from the ingredients that you want to compost. It takes you through a series of choices and questions. Following these through, you should end up at a green box with one or more composting methods listed in it. From this you continue to the relevant chapter, which will guide you through each method, in a clear and practical way.

Of course, once you've got started you may decide to modify or change your method and/or ingredients, so don't feel that you have to follow the advice of the flow diagram exactly!

Above Grass clippings rot down quickly. Too many can overwhelm a compost bin and are best recycled in other ways.

Left Vegetable peelings from the kitchen are good for the compost heap.

CHOOSING THE RIGHT METHOD FOR YOU

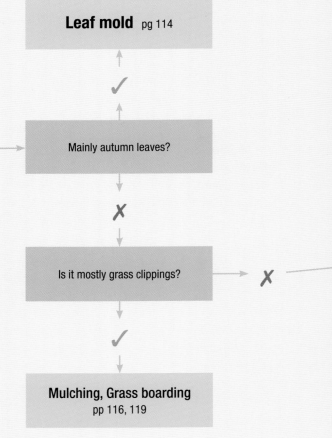

| Mainly food waste | → | Includes any of the following: fish, dairy, meat, cooked food? | ✓ |
| | | | ✗ |

Leaf mold pg 114

| Mainly garden waste | → | Mainly autumn leaves? |

Is it mostly grass clippings?   ✗

Mulching, Grass boarding
pp 116, 119

Working through this flow chart will lead you to the right method. The choice starts with the purple boxes – "Mainly food waste" or "Mainly garden waste." Follow the chart through to a green box where you will find one or two suitable methods of composting or an alternative way of recycling. These are described in detail further on in this book.

Do you want to produce compost?

✓ → Bokashi system
pp 120–121

✗ → Green cone
pp 112–113

Are you including more than 10% garden waste?

✗ → Worm composting, High-fiber composting pp 92–111, 118

✓

Are you concerned about perennial weeds?

✓ → Perennial weed bag or heap pg 130

✗ → Do you want to make compost quickly?

✗ → Cool composting
pp 51–52

✓ → Hot composting, Compost tumbler pp 53–55, 134–135

Do you have lots of woody waste?

✓ → Wildlife woodpile, Garden structures pg 126

Consider buying a shredder pg 129

4

MAKING COMPOST

This chapter covers what is perhaps regarded as the "traditional" composting method – where kitchen and garden waste is added to a compost bin. The "science" behind the composting process is explained in simple terms to give you an idea of what is going on in your bin and what you can do to help the composting process work effectively. This is followed by practical advice describing exactly what you have to do to make compost.

HOW COMPOSTING WORKS

Composting is a natural biological process carried out by millions of tiny creatures. Some of them, such as worms, you can see with the naked eye but the majority are microscopic.

Suitable creatures will arrive in your compost heap of their own accord if the conditions are right. They will eat their way through the organic material you have put in the bin, breaking it down further and further until all that remains is a wonderful dark brown earthy substance – compost. Find out more about the creatures that do all this excellent work in the section entitled "The creatures in your compost bin" (see page 156).

Composting takes place constantly in nature. Think about all those leaves that fall from the trees and plants that die. Have you ever wondered where they go? They are all consumed by worms and the myriad smaller "decomposers" and the goodness they contain is recycled back into the soil to help more plants grow. And so the natural cycle continues.

All you are doing as a home composter is managing this natural process so it happens in a tidier, more efficient fashion to give you the end product you want. You don't have to understand every detail of the process to make compost, but if you have some idea of what it's all about you are more likely to be successful and be able to

Below Nature is continually at work, decomposing and recycling living materials, including the leaves on the forest floor.

adjust the conditions in your compost heap to get a good end product.

THE NATURAL COMPOSTING PROCESS

The decomposition of organic (living) materials in compost has five main stages. These are more obvious to the observer in a hot compost heap, but still occur in cool composting methods (see pages 50–55 to find out more about hot and cool composting). Each stage involves the work of different organisms that are adapted to the specific conditions in the compost heap at that point. They come and go of their own accord.

Stage 1
Weeds, grass, kitchen scraps and other organic material you put in a compost bin will already have plenty of bacteria living on them. These bacteria start the decomposing process.

Stage 2
The bacteria and other micro-organisms multiply rapidly as they feed. Larger creatures such as insects and worms move in and start to feed on the decomposing organic material, breaking it into smaller and smaller pieces. All this activity releases energy as heat and the heap may begin to feel warm if a lot of material has been added at once. If the heap becomes too hot, then the worms and other larger creatures will move out until it cools down once again.

Above Worms are some of the larger creatures involved in the composting process.

Stage 3
This stage sees the most intense microbial activity and the heap may get really hot as activity increases. The bacteria involved at this stage are specially adapted to work at high temperatures. The heat generated may be enough to kill weed seeds, pests and disease organisms. Even if the heap does not heat up noticeably, the microbial activity can kill off many plant disease organisms that may have been added to the compost bin.

At this stage the volume of the stuff you put in the bin will be consumed and disappear at a dramatic rate.

Stage 4

All the creatures involved in composting need air to survive. At this stage air supplies within the heap may have been used up and suitable food supplies running low, so the composting activity slows down. A hot heap will cool down, allowing other bacteria and fungi to move in to take over from the heat-loving species and continue the work.

Stage 5

The compost will continue to decay slowly and after a period of time it will be ready to use. Don't worry if you find your compost bin full of earthworms, woodlice, ants and so on at this stage. They are part of the process and will continue working until there is nothing left – but you should have used the compost on your garden long before that!

Top right The number of worms in your compost heap can sometimes fluctuate, depending on the stage it is at.

Right Woodlice break down cellulose fibers in woody material, making it easier for other creatures to work on it.

WHAT IS NEEDED FOR EFFECTIVE COMPOSTING

Above Kitchen waste such as this is considered to be "green" waste, and rots down quickly.

RAW MATERIALS

What you regard as kitchen and garden "waste" is considered a good meal by the creatures that make compost. They need a balanced diet to stay healthy, to keep the composting process going and to produce a decent compost. Tender young materials, such as grass clippings, kitchen waste and young weeds provide nitrogen and speed the process along. These are known as "greens" in compost-speak.

At the other end of the scale are "browns" – tougher items such as older plant material and cardboard. Slower to decompose, these give the heap structure, maintain air pockets, and give body to the end product, compost. Many things you compost will be somewhere between the two, known as "green/browns."

If you fill your compost bin with roughly equal amounts of "green" and "brown" materials, all should be well and the result should be good-quality compost. You can find out which ingredients are good (and not so good) to add to your compost heap and which are green, brown or green/browns in the chapter entitled "What can I compost?" (see pages 60–77). There is no need to be very precise and you will soon learn from experience what makes good compost.

WATER

Composting creatures need moisture to live and work, but not too much of it. Too much water drives air out of the heap, and the air-loving composting creatures will drown. The bin will begin to smell, and turn slimy and unpleasant. However, if there is too little moisture, then very little noticeable composting will occur.

Green materials contain a high proportion of water and brown materials contain very little, so a mixture of the two is important. Some materials are a good balance on their own.

When adding dry, tougher ingredients to a compost bin, try to mix them with greens or water them before putting into the bin. A good tip is to add weeds and spent plants collected after a good shower of rain. Once the composting process has got going, you can test the water content. Squeeze a handful of the decomposing material in your fist; it should feel similar in dampness to a wrung-out sponge.

Use the lid of your compost bin to help manage the moisture content. In very wet weather, leaving the lid on will stop rain soaking the compost; in dry conditions, keeping the lid on will stop it drying out.

A compost bin must drain well so water cannot build up in it. Most bins don't have a base, so this is not a problem. If you are thinking of converting a garbage can or barrel for use as a compost bin, cut off the base or make plenty of drainage holes in it. The drainage aspect is important, but you also need to allow access and exits for all the useful creatures that will inhabit your bin and make it work.

Top left Compost that is this wet will tend to be airless and may smell unpleasant.

Left Material that is this dry will be very slow to compost. Add greens when adding dry material to your heap and water if necessary.

Right Ideally, compost should feel damp to the touch but should not ooze water when squeezed in the hand.

AIR

Air is another essential ingredient for making good compost. The composting creatures, large and small, need air to live (these are known as aerobic organisms). If a heap is very wet, air is excluded. Decomposition will occur, but it will be done by bacteria that don't need air (anaerobic organisms). The result will be a smelly, slimy mass, (not compost) and methane (one of the greenhouse gases responsible for global warming) will be produced.

Build air into a compost heap by adding browns amongst green materials to create air spaces. Egg cartons, toilet roll tubes, crumpled corrugated cardboard and scrunched up paper are useful if you are short of browns from the garden. It helps if you start your compost heap with a layer of twigs or branches in the bottom of your container so that the air can flow upwards from the base.

If a compost heap has slowed down due to lack of air, you can kick-start it again by "aerating" it in various ways:

- Make holes in the heap with a broom handle, right down to the bottom of the heap if possible. Or use a purchased aerating tool, which works in a similar way to a broom handle.

- Mix the whole heap up again. This is known as "turning" and you will find more information on this process on page 57.

Above A purpose-made aerating tool can be used to get more air into your compost heap, or you could try turning it over.

WARMTH

Composting activity is also affected by the temperature outside. It will slow down as the temperature drops and will almost come to a standstill when the weather is very cold. In warm weather the process will speed up.

You can regulate the temperature of a heap to some extent by placing the bin in a sunny spot, but it will still work (albeit more slowly) in the shade. You can also choose to make a compost heap that retains the heat liberated by the various composting organisms, speeding up the process considerably (see "How to make a 'hot' compost heap," page 55).

COLLECTING MATERIALS FOR YOUR COMPOST HEAP

As already mentioned, it is possible to compost a number of different materials generated by everyday life, some from the kitchen, from the household generally and from your garden.

KITCHEN MATERIALS

Collect vegetable peelings, coffee grounds, fruit cores and other kitchen waste in a container in the kitchen.

Below A sturdy brown paper liner keeps the can clean, and the liner can be deposited in the compost bin too.

Tips for no-smell, no-flies caddy use

- Empty the kitchen can every day or two in order to deter fruit flies and avoid smells.

- If you don't produce much kitchen waste, choose a small can so you have to empty it regularly.

- Add kitchen towels, paper tissues, toilet roll middles and the like to soak up excess moisture generated by the kitchen scraps.

- Don't empty liquids into the can.

- Consider using a brown paper liner or newspaper in your can. Simply remove the full paper liner and deposit the whole thing in your compost bin, where the paper liner will provide useful brown material to the heap.

Left Shredded paper can be added to a kitchen can to soak up excess moisture.

Top right Store some dry autumn leaves for use later as browns to balance your compost heap.

Bottom right Autumn leaves are heaped up on their own to make leaf mold.

HOUSEHOLD MATERIALS

Low-grade cardboard (such as cereal boxes), cardboard boxes, toilet roll middles and shredded paper can all be used in a compost heap to balance out the moisture content of fruit and vegetable peelings, grass clippings and other greens. Store these in a box or bag, to add to the compost bin as required.

GARDEN MATERIAL

Most garden "greens" are added straight to the compost bin, as they will start to rot anyway if stored.

As far as organic lawn care goes, it is best to leave the clippings on the lawn; worms will soon take these back down into the soil. If you prefer to compost your lawn clippings, and have large quantities to deal with, try leaving these on the lawn to dry out before raking them up. Once dry they can be stored for a while, if necessary, in an open plastic bin or bag, for use as required in your compost heap.

Deciduous leaves that fall in the autumn are also worth collecting and storing for later use. Large quantities are best made into leaf mold (see page 114) but also store some dry

Empty this container into the compost bin every day or so. There are all sorts of smart kitchen caddies on the market, or you can adapt a small pedal bin, use a plastic tub or just a simple bowl with a lid.

A purchased caddy used with a compostable liner is a good choice for those who prefer a neat and tidy look. If you use a compostable starch-based plastic-like liner, empty the contents out into the compost bin (the liner can go in, too) rather than throwing in a full liner with the top tied up. Sturdy brown paper liners are also available and should rot more quickly than the plastic-like ones.

leaves in a bin or bag for use in your compost over the coming year.

MATERIALS SOURCED FROM THE LOCALITY

Once you get started with compost-making, you may find that your garden or yard does not provide sufficient ingredients for your compost heaps. It makes sense to try and find other materials locally that you could use for compost, particularly from an environmental viewpoint, if this saves the materials from being transported to other sites to be recycled (or worse, put into landfill or incinerated).

Local public works may deliver autumn leaves to a designated area – or you may get permission to collect leaves locally. Go for leaves from parks and cemeteries, rather than those on the roadside. Shredded tree and shrub prunings are another useful resource that landscape contractors are often keen to give away (see page 129 for how to use them).

HOW TO MAKE COMPOST

How you actually make compost will depend on your circumstances: how much time you want to spend, the size and style of your garden, how fit you are, how much you have to compost, and how quickly you want to produce and use the end product.

QUICK OR SLOW COMPOSTING?

A well-managed "hot heap" can produce compost in as little as 12 weeks. This requires you to fill your compost bin in one go with the appropriate mix of ingredients, having chopped or shredded any larger items first. You will also need to turn the heap several times. This can be very satisfying if you have the time, the space and volume of ingredients.

At the other end of the scale is "cool composting," which may take 12–18 months to produce usable compost. In this case ingredients are added as and when they are available (still aiming to keep the balance of greens and browns). No other action is necessary.

Both methods can produce equally valuable compost. In practice most heaps are sometimes hot and sometimes cool.

Hot and cool composting compared

Hot heaps

- Relatively quick process
- More likely to kill weed seeds
- Many diseases killed
- Requires large volume of materials to be available at once
- Heap must be turned several times

Cool heaps

- Relatively slow process
- Less likely to kill weed seeds
- Some plant diseases killed
- Materials can be added as and when available
- Requires minimal management

HOW TO MAKE A "COOL" COMPOST HEAP

1 Put a 6 inch (10-20 cm) layer of twigs or branches at the bottom of the bin if you have them available. This is not vital if you don't have any to hand.

2 Start adding compostable materials to the bin. Remember that a successful compost heap needs a roughly balanced mix of green and brown materials.

When you put in fruit and vegetable waste from the kitchen, try to add roughly the same volume of "browns" (see page 43). This could be cereal boxes or toilet roll tubes, for example. Remember to scrunch up the cardboard to help maintain air gaps in the composting material. You may not be able to balance each "offering" you add to the bin, but try and average it out generally. You will learn by experience what works. The same applies to weeds, grass clippings and other compostable items from the garden. Balance grass clippings with cardboard, autumn leaves or tougher plant material.

3 Spread the ingredients out overthe whole area of the bin. A garden fork is useful for this or a long-handled hand fork if you don't add much to the bin at once.

Above A "Dalek"-type compost bin is simple to use and suits many garden situations.

4 As the composting process gets going, the level in the bin will go down. Compost will begin to form from the bottom up.

5 Keep filling your compost bin with material from the garden and kitchen as and when it is available.

6 After 6–12 months you have several choices of action. You could just keep on adding to this bin. If your compost bin has a door at the base, you may be able to scoop out some ready compost (see "When is it ready?," page 141). Alternatively you could start a new bin, leaving the first one to finish composting. Or, lift the bin off the heap to see how things are going. The upper layers should consist of material in various stages of breakdown. Put this back into the bin. At this stage you can adjust the mixture. If it is rather wet and slimy, mix in more browns. If everything is rather dry, add more greens, or water it.

The remaining compost that is ready for use can be employed immediately or you can cover it up and store until you need it.

Compost activators

A compost activator is simply something that gets the compost heap working. In general, if you add a good mix of green and brown materials there should be no need to add a specific activator.

Tender, quick-to-decompose materials such as grass clippings or comfrey leaves, are natural, cost-free activators. Comfrey is a vigorous herbaceous perennial (see photograph, right) whose leaves are rich in nitrogen and potassium, and can be cut several times a year to make a compost activator. They also make a good liquid feed, and can be mixed with leaf mold to make a rich potting mix. Comfrey "Bocking 14" is the best variety to grow for garden use.

Human urine can also be used as an activator in a compost heap; as it has a high salt content, it must be diluted by at least 1:10 and not applied in excess.

You can also buy activators, which are watered on or sprinkled as a powder as the bin is filled. Some types supply nitrogen in an easily accessible form to get the bacteria started, some supply enzymes and micro-organisms, while others claim to stimulate bacterial activity.

Some people feel that activators do make a real difference but the choice, ultimately, is yours. Organic gardeners would not use any activators that contain a chemical nitrogen fertilizer.

How compost heaps become hot

As plant wastes are broken down, the energy that went into making them is released in the form of heat. The heat build-up is a result of the oxidation of organic substances and the manufacture of carbon dioxide and water. Energy is released as molecular bonds are broken and reformed. Temperatures in the middle of a heap can reach up to 176°F (80°C)!

There is an initial phase of rapid microbial growth on the most readily available sugars and amino acids.

This phase is initiated by mesophilic organisms, which generate heat by their metabolism and raise the temperature to a point where their own activities are suppressed. Then a few thermophilic (heat-loving) fungi and bacteria continue the process, raising the temperature of the material within a few days.

Above Adding browns as well as greens will make your hot heap work more efficiently.

HOW TO MAKE A "HOT" COMPOST HEAP

1 Start with a compost bin with dimensions of about 3 feet (1 meter) high, wide and long.

2 Gather together sufficient compostable materials to fill the container. Aim for roughly equal volumes of green and brown materials.

3 Chop up or shred larger items, such as cabbage stalks, prunings and large plants (see "Shreddings and chippings" on page 129). Smaller pieces are easier for the composting creatures to work on.

4 Add alternating layers of greens and browns of 12 inches (30 cm) or so deep. You can just mix everything up together, but layering makes it easier to gauge green to brown proportions. Water the layers as you go if the materials are too dry.

5 Spread ingredients out evenly to the edges of the container and press down gently, but do not compact down.

6 Put the lid on or cover the heap. A compost "blanket," such as some woollen jumpers, a black plastic sack full of leaves or some polystyrene packaging, helps to keep the heat in.

7 After a few days (times will vary) you should feel warmth if you put your hand on the heap. If you stick an iron bar into a hot heap for a few minutes it can be too hot to handle when you pull it out. The heap may continue to heat up over a period of days and then will gradually begin to cool down.

8 Once the heap has cooled down, turn it (see page 57) to incorporate more air. At this stage you can also adjust the proportion of greens and browns, or add water if necessary.

9 At this point, the heap may heat up again, to a lesser extent. If it does, repeat step 8 to incorporate more air into the heap.

10 Leave your hot compost heap to mature (see "When is it ready?," page 141) before use. It is possible to produce finished compost in as little as 12 weeks, but it may take up to six months, depending on how fine a product you are aiming for.

CHOPPING AND SHREDDING

The smaller the bits of material that go into your compost bin, the faster they will compost. So if you have any particularly large, tough or chunky items it pays to reduce their size or at least damage them first. You can use pruning clippers if appropriate or simply bash the item with a brick. A sharp spade will chop through items such as Brussels sprout stems or corn cobs. To avoid jarring your shoulders, lay items to be chopped on the soil or grass, not on a hard surface. If you have large quantities of prunings to compost (from a hedge, for instance), shredding them first can be very useful.

Above A shredder reduces woody stems and branches to compostable proportions; you can either buy or hire a shredder if you choose.

SHREDDERS

A shredder will transform an ungainly heap of woody prunings, hedge trimmings and tough stems and stalks into a neat pile of shreddings that are ideal for adding to your compost heap, or for composting separately (see "Shredding and clippings," page 129).

There are many different types of shredders available – gas powered or electric, quiet or noisy, small to very large. It may be more worthwhile to rent a powerful shredder now and again rather than buying a small model, which will be less efficient and more time-consuming to use. Some local public works offer a shredding service.

Once you have access to a shredder, it can be tempting to shred everything in sight, but it is best to restrict this to tougher materials. If you shred everything, the compost heap will tend to compact too much and exclude air, slowing down the decomposing process.

TURNING AND AERATING

Simply speaking, turning a compost heap means removing the contents of a working compost bin then putting it back! This is best done using a garden fork. As you move the composting material, it gives you a chance to see how the process is progressing. You can break up solid lumps, mix drier stuff with wetter and adjust the mixture if necessary. Remixing it also incorporates more air into the heap, encouraging bacterial activity.

Turning is not essential, but it can speed up the composting process.

You can get more air into a compost heap by simply poking holes into the heap with a broom handle, or buy a "compost aerator" tool to do the job. This is not as efficient, but is much less effort than turning an entire heap.

COMPOST TUMBLERS

A compost tumbler is a compost bin that is designed to turn on an axle or just roll around so that the compost ingredients are mixed and turned. For more information on compost tumblers, see pages 134–135.

Above Turning and aerating with this compost tumbler is simple; when you feel the compost needs more air, rotate the bin on its axis several times to mix the contents well.

GETTING COMPOST OUT OF THE BIN

Once you've been composting for some time, you will want to use the fruits of your composting labors. Getting the compost out of your particular bin will depend on the kind of bin you have chosen to use.

Below The little door at the base of the bin allows you to see how the compost is progressing. You can also lift the bin completely off the heap (see the next three pictures) to expose the layers. This heap has ready-to-use compost at the bottom, and the rest is semi-composted with fresh material on top.

DALEK-TYPE BIN

The easiest way to get compost from a "Dalek"-type bin is to lift the whole bin off and put it to one side, leaving a tower of compost. Remove the semi-composted material from the top and put it back into the now-empty compost bin, leaving you with a pile of compost ready for use.

If you find that lifting the whole bin up is too difficult, you could try pushing it over onto its side, removing the ready compost and then pulling the bin back on top of the semi-composted material. Some

plastic bins have a door at ground level, which is intended to allow the removal of compost. However, because the door is generally rather small and the material at the bottom of the bin gets compacted, this is often not very easy. Lifting the bin off completely can be more effective (see photographs below).

BEEHIVE-TYPE BIN

Getting compost out of a beehive-type compost bin with stacking sections is very easy – simply remove the sections of the box and restack them next to the first bin as you empty it. You can put any semi-composted material from the first bin directly into the new stack to start another heap.

WOODEN OR WIRE-NETTING BINS

Wooden or wire-netting bins usually have one removable side for getting to the finished compost. If you only have one bin, pile any semi-composted material to one side ready to put back into your bin once you've emptied it of the usable compost.

5

WHAT CAN I COMPOST?

Many composters, particularly those who are new to the game, are likely to have some misconceptions about what can and cannot be composted. All sorts of items, from printed cardboard, through to citrus peels and poisonous plants are rejected, for any number of reasons (not all of which are valid). Many ideas about what is compostable seem to be passed down through the generations or over the garden fence! This chapter aims to encourage everyone to increase the range of items that they compost – not only will this lead to better compost heaps, but it will help to reduce the amount of rubbish going into landfill sites.

WILL IT COMPOST?

If you are having difficulty deciding what is compostable or not, then refer to the chart on the following pages. It lists a wide range of household and garden waste that will compost, and some examples of items that will not. The chart also outlines a number of items that perhaps one ought to avoid composting for various reasons, which will be given in the notes (also see below, "Should I put it on my compost heap?"). Use these notes as a guide when trying to decide whether or not to compost and what to compost.

If you are a keen recycler and are always on the lookout for more things to add to your compost heap, then the following chart might give you some fresh ideas. It will certainly help you reduce the amount of rubbish you need to put out for collection by the refuse collecting services.

SHOULD I PUT IT ON MY COMPOST HEAP?

In practice, it pays to be a bit selective about what you put on your compost heap. Some things, such as cat and dog feces, can transmit human pathogens and should be avoided. Woody prunings are very slow to rot and break down, but can be shredded and made into a separate slow heap. Cooked foods and meat and dairy products may attract vermin, but they can be pre-treated to avoid this risk (see pages 112–137 for other methods). These issues are highlighted in the "Caution" and "Notes" columns of the chart.

OTHER COMPOSTING METHODS

The traditional compost heap is not the only way to recycle garden and kitchen waste. The chart also covers worm composting (outlined on pages 92–111) and other composting methods (outlined on pages 112–137). Some materials are more suitable for one or another of the alternative methods.

"GREENS" AND "BROWNS"

Getting the right balance of "greens" and "browns" in your compost heap sounds daunting but guidance is at hand in the chapter entitled "Making Compost" (pages 38–59), which introduces the concept of "greens" and "browns" in relation to compost ingredients. Basically, green materials are quick to rot, but don't give the compost much body. Brown items are tougher, woodier materials that are slower to decay, but are essential for good compost. The trick is to get a good balance of both greens and browns in your compost heap.

Right Garden trimmings and dead-headed flowers can also go into your compost heap.

WHAT CAN I COMPOST?

The charts on the following pages outline what you can and can't (or shouldn't) put in your compost bin. For ease of reference, the chart has been divided into groups of materials: Plant materials; Animal products; Kitchen waste; Animal waste; Packaging and paper; and Miscellaneous items. The chart will also help you decide which type of composting method to use as well as providing further information and cautions in the notes.

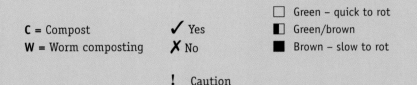

C = Compost ✓ Yes ☐ Green – quick to rot
W = Worm composting ✗ No ◨ Green/brown
 ■ Brown – slow to rot

! Caution

PLANT MATERIALS

Item	C	W	Notes
☐ Apple windfalls	!	✗	Large amounts of apples will stop a traditional compost heap working well. Instead of composting, store apples to feed birds through the winter. **Other methods:** Apple worm heap (see page 124); compost trench (see page 132).
◨ Carrot tops	✓	✓	These will not attract carrot root fly.
◨ Citrus peels	✓	!	Citrus peel is very acidic, and can upset a worm compost system if it makes up a high proportion of the material added.
◨ Potato and tomato plants	✓	✗	Blight-infected potato and tomato foliage can be composted safely. Add straight to the bin, cover with other materials and close the lid. Do not compost infected potato tubers or tomato fruits. Do not compost potato tubers and peelings that include an "eye" that

	Item	C	W	Notes
▮	Potato peelings and tubers	!	!	may be blight infected. New shoots may grow from these and could also carry potato blight, spreading the disease. Peelings from healthy tubers can be added to a compost bin and a worm bin. Whole potato tubers are quite resistant to decay and are not suitable for a worm bin.
▮	Rhubarb leaves	✓	✗	Although poisonous to eat, rhubarb leaves will not harm a compost heap; the compost produced will not harm plants.
■	Sweetcorn cobs	✓	!	May have to go through two or three compost heaps before they decay fully.
▢ ▮	Vegetable and fruit waste from garden	✓	✓	
▢ ▮	Vegetable and fruit waste from kitchen	✓	✓	Mix with low-grade paper to soak up excess liquid. Chop up tough stems of Brussels sprouts, cabbages etc. **Other methods:** High-fiber heap (see page 118).
▢ ▮ ■	Plant debris and waste flowers, leaves, old bedding plants etc.	✓	!	Chop up tough stems. **Other methods:** Compost trench (see page 132).

Item	C	W	Notes
▪ Fern	✓	✗	Good source of potash; makes compost more suitable for acid-loving plants.
☐ Comfrey leaves	✓	✗	Good activator, rich in potash and nitrogen.
☐ Seaweed	!	✗	Composts well and is a traditional source of fertility, but collecting it can remove valuable wildlife habitats. Only use seaweed from your locality, that has been recently washed up, and then only in small quantities.
☐ Flowers ▪ *Purchased bunches*	✓	✓	Chop up tough stems; compost paper wrappings.
▪ Houseplants	✓	✓	Rootball and compost can also be added if broken up first (though it will not compost any further). Check for white, vine weevil grubs in the root ball. These pests should be squashed or fed to the birds.
▪ Leaves *Autumn deciduous*	!	✗	Store drier leaves in sacks and use to balance excess greens next season. Make the rest into leaf mold. **Other methods:** Leaf mold (see page 114).
Leaves *Evergreen*	!	✗	Mix well with other other ingredients as these take a long time to break down.

Item	C	W	Notes
■ Moss	✓	✗	Slow to rot; mix with other ingredients. Do not use if taken from a lawn recently treated with weedkiller.
☐ Nettles	✓	✗	Young leaves are a good compost activator. Roots may not rot in a single composting. Other methods: Weed bag (see page 130); "nasty weed" heap (see page 130).
☐ Grass clippings	✓	✗	Very quick to decay, these make a good activator, but particularly need to be balanced with "browns." Don't compost clippings from the first two cuts after treating a lawn with weedkiller. **Other methods:** Grass boarding (see page 119); mulching (see page 116–117); leave on lawn.
◧ Hay	!	✗	Hay should be soaked well before adding to the compost heap; spoiled hay is best for this purpose. **Other methods:** Mulching (see page 116–117).
■ Straw	✓	✗	Old, weathered straw is best. Fresh straw is very dry and must be well soaked or mixed with wetter ingredients.
☐ Pest-infested plant ◧ material ■	!	✗	Pests that only live on living plant material will not survive a compost heap. Pests that live on dead and decaying plant material or have a resistant stage are more likely to survive. **Other methods:** Weed bag (see page 130); compost trench (see page 132).

	Item	C	W	Notes
☐ ◨ ■	Diseased plant material	!	!	Plants with soil-borne diseases such as white rot on onions, brown rots on fruits, wilts of tomatoes and cucurbits, and clubroot of brassicas are best not added to a compost heap. These types of disease can survive for many years in the soil and are unlikely to be killed off. Many other common diseases, such as mildew, only survive on living plant material so infected plants can be composted safely.
☐ ◨ ■	Poisonous plants	✓	✗	Plants that are poisonous to eat will not harm a compost heap; the compost produced will not harm plants. Take care not to inhale dust or fumes when shredding poisonous plants..
☐ ◨	Weeds *annual*	✓	!	Try to pull up weeds before seeds form. Some weed seeds will be killed in the composting process, particularly if it heats up. If your compost tends to grow weeds, see page 142 for "Using weedy compost." Keep compost covered to prevent weed seeds blowing in.
◨	Weeds *perennial, roots and tops*	!	✗	Including bindweed, lambsquarters, pigweed, buckhorn plantain, crabgrass. **Other methods:** Weed bag (see page 130); and Nasty weed heap (see page 130)
◨	Japanese knotweed	!	✗	This is a very invasive weed. There are best practices for its disposal (see page 131).

PLANT MATERIALS

Item	C	W	Notes
■ Christmas trees ▉	!	✗	Shred before adding to a compost heap. Be cautious when adding large quantities of this material. **Other methods:** Composting woody waste (see page 129).
▉ Pruning and hedge clippings *evergreen, conifer and deciduous*	!	✗	Young, supple items can be added to a compost heap. Take care when using compost if you have added thorny prunings. Thorns take a long time to compost and may still be sharp. **Other methods:** Shredding compost (see page 129).
■ Sawdust and woodshavings	!	✗	Very dry, high in carbon and tend to exclude air. Mix well with wet greens, and only use in relatively small amounts (see Nitrogen robbery page 149).
■ Dead wood *branches, twigs and shrubs*	!	✗	Dead wood is much harder to shred than recently cut living wood. **Other methods:** Wildlife heap; plant supports (see page 126).

KITCHEN WASTE

Item	C	W	Notes
Bread	✗	✗	Tends to grow molds rather than compost. If you do want to try composting bread, crumble it up and mix with moist ingredients. **Other methods:** Bokashi (see pages 120–121).
☐ Tea leaves and bags	✓	✓	Some tea bags have a very small amount of plastic in them, which is not immediately obvious. If the packaging doesn't say "tea bags compostable," then don't put the bag itself into the compost. The contents can be emptied, or even better use loose leaf where possible.
☐ Coffee grounds	✓	✓	Paper coffee filters can also be composted.
Food *cooked leftovers*	!	✗	Cooked food does not compost particularly well. Mix with uncooked materials and items that will allow air into it. May attract bluebottles and vermin such as foxes and rats. Can make heap smell. **Other methods:** Bokashi (see pages 120–121); Green Cone (see page 123).
Oil *olive oil, vegetable oils etc.*	!	✗	Composting is not a good way to dispose of cooking oils. Oil-soaked paper or cardboard can be composted.

ANIMAL PRODUCTS

Item	C	W	Notes
Bones – meat and fish	✗	✗	May attract bluebottles and vermin such as foxes and rats. Can make heap smell unpleasant. **Other methods:** Bokashi (see pages 120–121); Green Cone (see page 123).
Meat and fish scraps	✗	✗	May attract bluebottles and vermin such as foxes and rats. Can make heap smell unpleasant.**Other methods:** Bokashi (see pages 120–121); Green Cone (see page 123).
Dairy products *milk, cheese, yoghurt etc.*	✗	✗	May attract vermin such as bluebottles, foxes and rats. Can make heap smell unpleasant. **Other methods:** Bokashi (see pages 120–121), Green Cone (see page 123).
Eggshells	✓	✓	Eggshells do not compost as such, but will eventually break down into tiny pieces. They may remain visible in finished compost, but this is not a problem. Baking shells in the oven will make them more brittle and therefore easier to break down into tiny bits.

ANIMAL WASTE

Item	C	W	Notes
Cat litter	✗	✗	Although some brands of cat litter say they can be composted, once it has been used there is a health risk to anyone handling it.
Dog feces	✗	✗	Toxocara is a dangerous disease that can be found in dog and cat poo and can be passed on to humans if handled.
■ Hair, *human and pet*	✓	✗	Very slow to compost but adds useful nutrients.
▮ Manure *from livestock and pets with straw, hay or paper bedding*	✓	✗	Only compost manures from vegetarian or omnivorous animals and pets.
■▮ Manure *from livestock and pets with wood shavings bedding*	!	✗	Use only as a small proportion of the compost heap. Risk of nitrogen robbery (see page 149).
■ Diapers *disposable*	✗	✗	Not generally recommended to compost disposable diapers. Some types claim to be biodegradable and may produce compost when balanced with a high number of "greens." Use urine-soaked diapers only.
☐ Urine	✓	✓	Dilute first, approximately 1:10 with water. Research (limited) indicates that there appears to be no need to be concerned about pharmaceuticals and hormones excreted with the urine.

PACKAGING AND PAPER

Item	C	W	Notes
■ **Cardboard boxes** *(see also cardboard packages)*	✓	✗	Plain and color printed cardboard can be composted. Crumple it up into rough balls – flat sheets will exclude air. A good counterbalance to excess "greens." Remove any packing tape and staples. A large box can make a good short-term compost bin. **Other methods:** Grass boarding (see page 119).
■ **Cardboard food packages** *cereal boxes, tubes from kitchen towel and toilet rolls*	✓	✓	Plain and color printed cardboard can be composted. Check juice and other cartons that may include a layer of plastic. **Other methods:** High-fiber heap (see page 118).
■ **Egg cartons**	✓	✓	Their shape help keeps air in the heap; a good counterbalance to kitchen waste. **Other methods:** High-fiber heap (see page 118).
■ **Food and drinks cartons**	!	✗	Do not compost longlife cartons that have an aluminium foil lining. Other cartons may have a plastic lining, but this can always be removed once the composting process is complete.
■ **Newspaper**	!	!	Large quantities are best sent for recycling. Newspaper is good for absorbing excess moisture, particularly in a worm bin. It can also be used as a weed control mulch in the garden. **Other methods:** Garden mulch (see pages 116–117).
■ **Paper** *high quality*	!	!	Environmentally, this is best sent for recycling, but it can be added to a compost heap. Scrunch it up into balls first. Flat sheets don't allow air movement in the heap. Shredded paper can be added, but scrunched is better.

Item	C	W	Notes
■ **Paper** *low-quality including paper bags, kitchen towels (see also newspaper)*	✓	✓	Good for absorbing excess moisture. Scrunch up before adding to allow air movement in the heap. Do not add kitchen paper if it has been used to mop up bleach or other chemical products. **Other methods:** High-fiber heap (see page 118).
■ **Junk mail**	!	!	Some leaflets contain plastic. Tear a page to check before composting. Both black-and-white and colored printing can be composted. Scrunch it up rather than adding as flat sheets.
Plastic-style carrier bags and packaging *labelled biodegradable and compostable*	!	✗	The whole area of compostable and recyclable "plastic" packaging is complex, and the current terminology misleading or at least confusing so it is best to avoid adding plastic-style materials to your heap.
Plastic bottles	✗	✗	Will not compost; recycle with other household waste.
Plastic wrap	✗	✗	Not biodegradable.
Chip bags	✗	✗	Not biodegradable.
Glass	✗	✗	Not biodegradable. Recycle.
Beverage cans	✗	✗	Not biodegradable. Recycle.
Tin cans	✗	✗	Not biodegradable. Recycle.

MISCELLANEOUS ITEMS

Item	C	W	Notes
Wool, cotton and other natural fiber clothing	✓	✓	All natural fiber materials can be composted, although care should be taken if a garment has a printed logo on it.
Ashes *coal and coke*	✗	✗	Coal ash does not compost and it contains high levels of sulphur and other impurities. Small quantities that may be mixed with wood ash can be put in a compost bin.
Ashes *wood*	✓	✓	A good source of minerals, wood ash (and unburned charcoal) from lumpwood barbeque charcoal is fine; do not use ash from briquettes.
Soil	!	!	There is no need to add soil to a heap. Soil on roots of weeds and plants is fine, but avoid adding large clumps and clods.
Stones and pebbles	✗	✗	These are not compostable since they are non-living materials.

6 A HOME FOR YOUR COMPOST

The days are long gone when a compost heap meant an untidy pile of debris at the bottom of the garden, held together with various recycled bits and pieces. There is, of course, nothing wrong with making compost that way, but it doesn't suit everyone or every garden. Fortunately, the range of DIY and ready-made composting containers is such that there should be one to suit everyone's taste, lifestyle and garden. This chapter deals with containers for making what we call "traditional compost." Other sections of this book cover compost tumblers, worm composting and various methods of making compost. Containers suitable for those methods are described in the particular sections.

BUYING A COMPOST BIN

There are numerous kinds of compost bins made of plastic or wood on the market, at a wide range of prices. If possible, try before you buy to be sure that you like what you are getting, and it meets the criteria listed on the next page. However, as the greatest range of composting bins is available via mail order and online this isn't always possible. Also ask your local public works; these days many local governments are keen to help promote composting and often offer their residents compost bins at low prices.

As a newcomer to composting, you are probably best off buying a simple no-frills plastic or wooden bin, or making your own (see pages 84–90).

FEATURES OF A GOOD COMPOST BIN

Whether bought or homemade, there are features that make some compost bins better than others – longer lasting perhaps or easier to use. Ultimately though, it is what you do that makes the biggest difference to the quality of the compost produced. The most important feature is that you like the bin and that it suits you, your lifestyle and your garden. If you

Below There are many types of compost bin available. Choose one you like.

don't like your compost bin you will be less inclined to use it, and more likely to hide it away in an inaccessible spot.

What is it made of?

A compost container can take quite a battering when being filled and emptied, and a full load of compost is quite a weight, so make sure your container is sturdy enough to stand up to constant use.

Wood is an appropriate material for a compost bin, as it is itself a natural product. It is a renewable resource and will, in time, decay back into the soil. Wood is strong, provides some insulation, and it "breathes," so the compost is less likely to get too wet.

There are a few wooden boxes on the market or you can make your own (see pages 84–90). You can be creative with the design, and the wood can be stained (with a non-toxic product) in a color of your choice. It makes sense to use recycled wood if possible – old pallets for example or whatever you can find locally.

Wood preservatives may be an issue here. Even though some preservatives are more "environmentally friendly" than others, none really fit in with the ethos of organic gardening. Our advice would be to use untreated wood, accepting that the bin will rot eventually.

While wooden bins tend to be square and on the large side, plastic bins (usually made from recycled plastic) come in a wider range of shapes and sizes, to suit all sorts of gardens. Homemade compost containers can also be constructed from straw bales, wire mesh fixed around four posts and lined with cardboard, sheets of corrugated metal and

Above A double-bay wooden compost box – the front slats can be removed for easy access.

many other reused materials, including a plastic garbage can with the bottom cut off.

How heavy is it?

If the compost bin needs to be lifted up to access the compost, then make sure you get one that you can lift. In a windy spot, a heavier bin is less likely to blow over when it is relatively empty.

Solid or slatted sides

Air is an essential component of good composting, but this is built into the heap as you make it. A compost bin does not need any holes or gaps in the sides. Large gaps allow the material to dry out and heat to escape; they are not particularly effective at getting air into the centre of the heap where it is needed. If you have a wire mesh container, line it with flattened out cardboard boxes.

Volume and dimensions

The size of bin you choose will depend on how much material you have to compost, rather than the size of your garden or of your family (although these elements may be linked). About 200 gallons (750 liters) or 1 cubic yard has traditionally been recommended as a minimum for fast, hot composting. This is a good size for a large garden. Most bins on the market average 50-90 gallons (200-350 liters) and are appropriate for most households and gardens of today. Models smaller than this are unlikely to make compost satisfactorily.

Keeping it covered

A lid or some sort of cover is useful as it can help regulate the moisture content in the bin. A cover also prevents weed seeds from blowing in. The lids on some models are much easier to get off than others. It helps if it doesn't blow away easily!

Base

It is important that excess moisture can drain from a compost heap – so most compost bins do not have or need a base. If there is a base it must have good drainage to allow excess moisture to seep away and worms should be able to get into the heap from below.

Rat-proofing

Rats can eat their way into a plastic or wooden compost bin if they feel so inclined. To make a bin rat-proof, you need to line it (including the base) with wire mesh. For more information about rats in compost heaps, see page 184.

Static or mobile

Some bins are free-standing and easy to move. Others have stakes in the ground for support, so are not easy to move. Choose to suit your circumstances.

Filling the bin

A reasonable sized opening at the top is important. Trying to deposit a forkful of compost material through a narrow opening is not easy.

Getting it out

Some compost bins have a small access door at ground level, so you can scoop out the finished compost. This is really only practical for small quantities, so a bin without an access door is fine. You just lift it off. Wooden bins may have one side that is removable, which makes it very easy to empty the bin.

Right With so many different designs of bin to choose from, you are sure to find a suitable home for your kitchen waste.

MAKING YOUR OWN COMPOST BIN

It is possible to make your own compost bin from a number of materials. Below you will find several suggestions, some of which are illustrated. Perhaps the easiest to make is the large plastic dustbin composter – simply cut off the bottom of a large dustbin, turn it upside down and use the lid as a cover for your composter.

STRAW BALE BIN

If space is not too much of an issue, then you can easily construct a fairly large compost bin using straw bales as the frame. Straw is a natural material and in a year or two will break down and turn into compost itself. This particular shape requires nine bales but you could make a smaller or larger container depending on your own requirements.

1 Place six straw bales into a square on the ground in a suitable location. Place the other three bales to make sides and a back to your compost bin, as shown here.

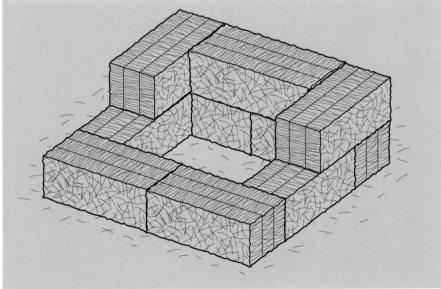

2 You can then use the straw container as you would any other compost bin, filling it with material. Cover it with a heavy plastic sheet or tarpaulin.

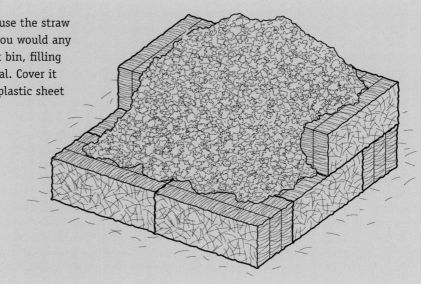

3 After a year or two, when the bales have rotted so much that they can no longer hold the heap together, you will need to replace them. Cut the string from the decaying bales and add the straw to your next compost heap (or use it as a mulch on the garden).

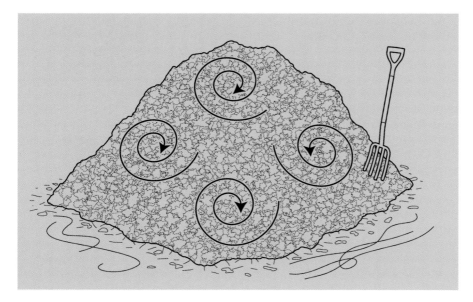

POST AND WIRE BIN

A post and wire bin is particularly useful for making leaf mold but is perfectly good for conventional composting as well.

You will need four sturdy posts, some chicken wire a yard (meter) wide, some fence staples and some cardboard with which to line your finished bin.

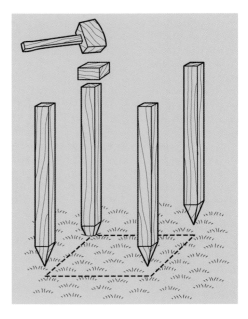

1 In a suitable location, mark out where you want your bin to go – 1 yard (meter) square is a good size.

2 Using a hammer, drive the posts into the ground at the corners of your square. Make sure that they are as vertical as possible and that they are driven in deep enough to be safe and sturdy.

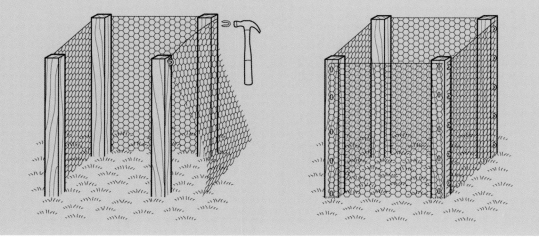

3 Cut three panels of chicken wire of 1 yard (meter) wide and the same height as your poles. Using the fence staples, nail each of these to one of three sides.

4 A fourth panel of wire finishes off the container. Line the whole thing with flattened cardboard boxes. They can be held in place if necessary with string ties through the cardboard fixed on to the wire mesh.

RECYCLED WOODEN PALLETS

Old pallets can be used to make an excellent one- or two-bay compost bin for a large garden. The pallets can be tied together with sturdy string or roughly nailed. Remember to leave one side so that it is easy to remove to allow access. Stuff sheets of cardboard or other material between the two layers of wood that make up the pallets.

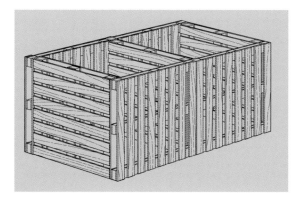

DIY SECTIONAL COMPOST BIN

The following instructions describe how to make a moveable, wooden compost box consisting of identical interlocking sections that are stacked one on top of the other. As you fill the bin, sections can be added to the box; as the contents decay the volume will decrease, so the top sections of the box can be taken off and used to build up a new container. Make a few extra sections and you will have a very flexible composting system. Keep the rain out with a wooden lid or plastic sheet.

Size

These instructions will make a compost box 30 x 30 x 30 inches (76 x 76 x 76 cm). The dimensions can be adjusted to suit the materials available, making it ideal for using reclaimed timber such as floorboards or pallets. The example given uses boards that are 3 inches (7.5 cm) wide but they can be any width you like, as long as all the boards in one section are the same width. Adjust the length of the corner blocks to suit (approximately ¾ inch (2 cm) shorter than the width of the board).

Materials and tools

To make one section of the box you will need the following:
- two 30 inch (76 cm) wooden boards, 3 inches (7.5 cm) wide, minimum ⅗ inch (1.5 cm) thick
- two 28 inch (72 cm) wooden boards, 3 inches (7.5 cm) wide, minimum ⅗ inch (1.5 cm) thick
- four 2 inch (5 cm) x 2 inch (5 cm) wooden corner blocks, 2¼ inches (5.5 cm) long
- twenty 1½ inch (3.6 cm) screws, size number 8
- screwdriver, drill, and saw

Total materials for 10 sections:
100 feet (30 meters) of 3 inch (7.5 cm) x ⅗ inch (1.5 cm) timber; 7½ feet (2.2 meters) of 2 x 2 inch (5 x 5 cm) timber; 220 screws

.

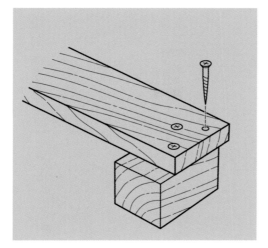

1 Cut two boards, each 30 inches (75 cm) long and two boards, each 28 inch (72 cm) long. Cut four lengths of 2¼ inches (5.5 cm) from the 2 x 2 inch (5 cm x 5 cm) timber to make the corner blocks.

2 Take one of the two shorter boards and place it in position on two of the corner blocks. The ends of the board should be flush with the blocks; the blocks should be offset so that they project ¾ inch (2 cm) beyond the edge of the board, as shown in the diagram above.

3 Hold the board in position on the blocks. Drill three holes, 1 inch (3 cm) deep at one end of the board, through the board and into the block below. Fasten with three screws.

4 Repeat steps 4 and 5 at the other end of the board.

5 Now repeat steps 4–6 with the second shorter 28 inch (72 cm) board. For the next stage you may need someone to hold the pieces while you fix them together.

6 Stand the two shorter boards (with blocks attached) on their ends, approximately 30 inches (75 cm) apart, with the protruding ends of the blocks away from you. Place a 30 inches (75 cm) board on top of these vertical boards to form the third side of the section. Ensure that the ends of the longer board are flush with the outer edges of the vertical boards.

7 Drill and screw each end of the 30 inch (75 cm) board, as in step 5. Use two screws only this time.

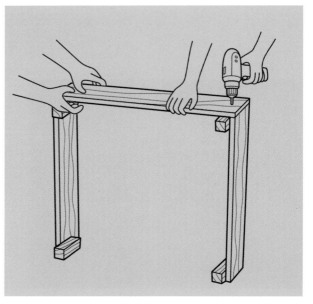

8 Turn the section over so that the unfinished side is uppermost. Place the second 30 inch (75 cm) board across between the shorter boards as before. Position squarely and drill and screw as in step 7.

9 You have now completed the first section of your compost box. Continue making sections until you have as many as you need.

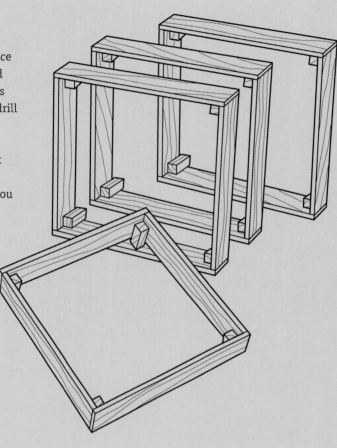

TWO-BAY WOODEN COMPOST BIN

Reclaimed and recycled wood has been used to make this two-bay compost bin. Use whatever materials you have to hand to construct a similar bin. This design is traditionally called a New Zealand box. Each bay is a 3 foot (1 meter) cube, which promotes hot composting if you have sufficient material.

WHERE TO PLACE YOUR COMPOST BIN

There are a number of basic requirements to keep in mind when placing your compost bin in your garden. First and foremost it must be outdoors! It also needs to be accessible all year round, even in the winter. If you don't like to look at it, put it behind a screen or a trellis. A decent path to the compost bin is useful so you can use it regularly, particularly in winter. It is also important to have a bit of room around the bin so that you have space to work when filling and emptying.

It is preferable to have your compost bin on bare ground (or lawn) so any liquid produced by the decomposing material can drain away. If your only option is to place it on a hard surface, you can still make perfectly good compost. Put a thick layer of newspaper or cardboard in the bottom of the bin to soak up as much liquid as possible, although it is likely that the slabs beneath will be stained. A sunny site for your compost bin is also preferable since the sun will speed up the compost process, but this is not essential.

Above If you don't like the look of your container you can hide it behind some garden trellis and pot plants.

PERMANENT SPOT OR MOVE IT AROUND?

The ground under a compost heap will be very rich after a year or so. You can make use of this fertility by moving the bin elsewhere and growing zucchini, pumpkins or beets for example, on the spot. You can also grow vegetables around a compost bin to take advantage of the fertility of the soil in the surrounding area. As it is not advisable to grow the same vegetables in the same place every year, it makes sense to be able to move the compost bin to different areas of the garden.

7

WORM COMPOSTING

Worm composting involves keeping worms of particular species in a container (a proprietary worm bin or a homemade version) and feeding them kitchen and some garden waste. They convert these materials into beautiful dark, crumbly compost that is rich in nutrients. The whole process is simple and effective – and can be interesting and fun too, particularly for children. The idea is not a new one. Worms have been used to assist in composting in the past, but there was little understanding of why they were so effective. Now recent studies worldwide have shown that worm composting has many benefits, not only for individual households, but also in large-scale agriculture and industry.

Left Worm compost is a nutrient-rich material that is good for top-dressing plants grown in containers, such as this dwarf peach tree.

Right A three-tiered worm composter conveniently sited close to the kitchen door.

nutrient-rich (see "How worms work," page 97) and has a good water-holding capacity. In addition, worm bins often produce a liquid, which can be collected and used diluted as a feed for house or garden plants.

WHY WORM COMPOSTING?

For the person with little or no garden, worm composting can be the ideal alternative to making garden compost. A worm compost bin can be compact and self-contained and the process is not smelly. As a consequence this system is suitable for use both indoors or out (or it can be moved between the two). You can fit one into the smallest garden or backyard or put one on a balcony.

Once set up, a worm bin takes little time and effort to maintain and, as the worms require feeding little and often, it is ideal for processing daily kitchen waste.

Even if you have a large garden and compost heaps, you may still like to add a worm bin to your recycling. It keeps working in winter if protected from the cold, so can be useful for dealing with kitchen waste all year round. The resulting worm compost is very

Advantages of a worm compost bin

- Can be small and unobtrusive.

- Once set up, it takes little effort to maintain.

- Can be moved around, and kept indoors or out.

- Thrives on a regular supply of kitchen waste.

- Will continue to work in winter if kept warm.

- Produces a high-quality organic compost and sometimes a rich liquid feed.

HOW TO START

All you need to start worm composting is a suitable container (which you can make yourself or buy), compost worms, suitable bedding material and some kitchen waste.

COMPOSTING WORMS

The worms used in a worm compost bin are those that live naturally in the garden in heaps of decaying vegetation and compost heaps. They are not normally found in the soil. The two most commonly used in worm composters are red wigglers (*Eisenia fetida*) and red worms (*Lumbricus rubellus*). It is likely that you will get a mixture of the two when you purchase worms for your worm composter (see photograph left).

HOW WORMS WORK

For success with your worm composter, it helps to understand how a worm works. Most of the inside of a worm is taken up by its digestive system – a tube running the length of its body. It takes food in at one end and "casts" come out the other end. These casts are worm manure, but are called worm compost. Secretions in the worm's intestinal tract concentrate nutrients and make them more available for plants to take up – hence the extra value of worm compost as fertilizer.

Worms don't have noses or lungs, but breathe through their skin. This means that

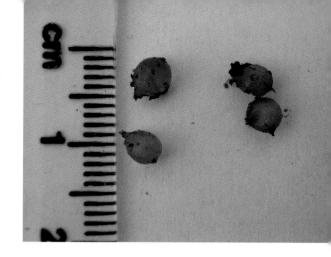

Above These tiny lemon-shaped cocoons each contain up to eight baby worms.

they need to be kept moist to survive. The mucus they produce in these conditions also helps them to move. Worms don't have eyes either, but can still sense light and always move away from it.

GETTING YOUR WORMS

To start a garbage-can-sized worm bin off quickly and easily, you need a lot of worms – ideally about 1,000 (1 lb or 500 g). You can start off with fewer, but will then have to wait until their numbers increase before the system works well.

If you buy a worm bin, the worms may be supplied with it. Otherwise, you can buy them via mail order or online from specialist suppliers or in fishing shops (where they are sold as bait). Specialist suppliers are likely to provide the most efficient worms, as they will have been selected specifically for this job.

An alternative is to collect worms from garden compost and manure heaps. Don't use soil-burrowing worms that are unearthed when you dig over the soil – these are not the right ones to use in a wormery.

An effective worm bin should:

- Have a large surface area relative to its volume.

- Keep worms in the dark.

- Keep the contents moist without letting in rain.

- Have good drainage.

- Allow good air circulation.

- Provide insulation against extremes of heat and cold.

- It does not need to be worm proof. Worms will not try to escape if the conditions are right.

WHAT WORMS NEED

A worm bin must provide suitable conditions for the worms to live, eat and breed. It is important to keep them moist, but definitely not waterlogged otherwise they will drown. When kitchen waste is added, a lot of liquid will usually be produced and this must be able to drain away – either into the ground or into a container for use as liquid feed. The liquid is a very valuable source of nutrients and can be used in a diluted form to feed plants and houseplants.

Worms also need air in order to survive and prefer to work near the surface of the material in the bin. The most efficient worm bins therefore have a large surface area relative to their volume.

Worms work best when the temperature is kept fairly constant. A temperature of around 66°F (19°C) is ideal; anything between 54-77° F (12-25°C) is fine. Too cold and the worms will slow down; too hot and they will become fatigued or dry out and die. Some worm bins are insulated to help maintain a healthy temperature. If your outdoor bin does not have good insulation built in, keep it out of direct sunlight in summer and cover it in

winter with an old carpet or bubble wrap, for example.

Alternatively, if the weather is very severe, bring the worm compost bin into an outbuilding such as a garage, shed or even inside to an all-season porch or utility room, in order to guarantee their survival.

Above A good mix of greens and browns is vital to the success of your worm composter.

TYPES OF WORM COMPOST BINS

There are various types of worm bins available through shops, mail order and online, but you can make your own worm bin out of second-hand or recycled containers. Ready-made containers will often include full instructions and everything you need to get started. They may even include worms.

MATERIALS

Most worm bins are made of plastic or untreated wood. Plastic bins retain more moisture so good drainage is particularly vital to keep the worms from becoming waterlogged. Many plastic bins have a convenient tap at the bottom to drain off the excess liquid. Worm bins made from wood tend to be easier to manage as some moisture can evaporate, and little or no excess liquid may be produced from these.

Above A large plastic planter or bucket can be used as a worm bin, as long as there are holes in the bottom. Cover with a lid of some sort.

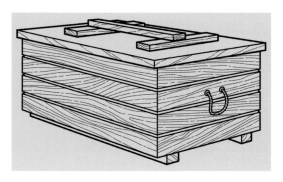

Above A wooden crate or packing box can also be used as a suitable worm container.

DESIGN

The simplest worm bins consist of a single container for the worms and waste, with a lid to keep out light and rain. Holes in the bottom allow excess liquid to drain away. This can be collected in a tray or, if the worm bin is kept in the garden, allowed to seep into the soil. Alternatively, a container with a solid base can have a sump to collect the liquid, with a tap to allow it to be drained off.

This type of bin has one main disadvantage – it is not easy to get out the worm compost without emptying the whole thing. Tiered worm bins, consisting of three or four stacked trays, get round this problem by allowing the worms to migrate upwards through holes in the base of each tier. When the lowest tier is full of worm-free compost it is removed and emptied.

Above A tiered worm composter allows for easy access to the finished compost in the bottom layer.

Above This type of worm composter often has a tap near the bottom in order to drain off excess moisture. Use the diluted nutrient-rich liquid to feed potted plants and other plants in the garden.

Above This tiered worm composter has been wrapped around with insulating material to keep the worms warm and working in cold weather.

MAKING AND SETTING UP YOUR OWN WORM BIN

The best time to start a worm bin is in late spring or early summer. The rising temperature will encourage breeding and feeding. Although it is possible to buy a number of different kinds of commercially produced worm bins, it is also quite easy to make your own from readily available materials and boxes. Suitable candidates for conversion are: plastic garbage cans, plastic rain barrels, plastic crates, wooden boxes and styrofoam fish boxes.

MAKING A WORM COMPOST BIN FROM A PLASTIC BIN

An ordinary plastic garbage can is easy to convert into a worm compost bin.

1 Choose a wide-necked garbage can with a lid. Drill two rows of drainage holes 1 inch (2.5 cm) up from the base and add another row of air holes at the top.

2 Place a 4 inch (10 cm) layer of gravel and/or coarse sand in the base. Add some sort of divider that will also allow drainage, such as strips of wood or a board with large holes drilled in it. This will prevent the worms and compost mixing with the sand or gravel.

3 Add a layer of damp newspaper followed by around 6 inches (15 cm) of bedding material. Place the worms on the bedding. Suitable bedding materials include leaf mold, garden compost, shredded newspaper or cardboard or coir, or a mixture of these. Make sure the bedding layer is thoroughly moist. When you squeeze some in your hand, moisture should just drip between your fingers.

4 Spread a thin layer of chopped kitchen waste over half the surface and cover it all with a thick layer of newspaper or cardboard.

5 Leave undisturbed for a week or two while the worms settle in. As the worms start eating through the waste you can add more food.

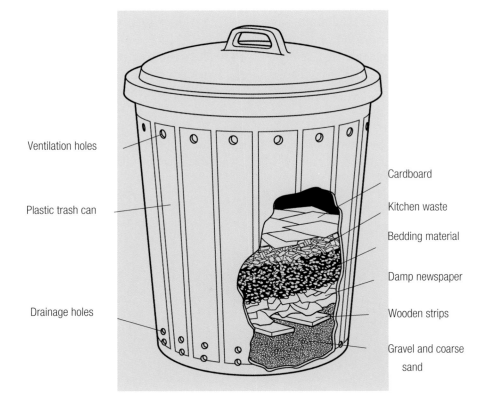

Ventilation holes

Plastic trash can

Drainage holes

Cardboard

Kitchen waste

Bedding material

Damp newspaper

Wooden strips

Gravel and coarse sand

MAKING A WORM BIN FROM OTHER RECYCLED MATERIALS

SHALLOW WOODEN BOX

Shallow wooden boxes can make ideal worm composters, although you should make sure that the wood is untreated.

1 Use discarded wooden boxes or build your own – ideal dimensions are 24 x 40 x 12 inches(60 x 100 x 30 cm) deep.

2 If the box already has slats it will provide natural drainage. If not, drill some holes in the bottom and set on a tray to catch the liquid or on the soil if desired.

3 Line with damp newspaper and fill with bedding (see step 3, page 103 regarding bedding), then add the worms.

4 Cover the surface with damp newspaper or a layer of cardboard, with a sheet of black plastic on top to block out the light and shield from rain.

PLASTIC CRATE

Plastic stacking crates are readily available and are very cheap to buy. You will need to drill holes in your crate.

1 Buy or use a plastic crate you already have. If possible buy two lids. Drill drainage holes in the base of the crate and some air holes around the top (much like the plastic garbage can, page 103).

2 Place the crate on one of the lids to act as a tray and use the other lid loosely over the top of the crate.

3 Continue as for steps 3–6, page 103, adding bedding and worms. Cover with the extra lid.

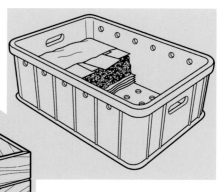

DIY INSULATED WORM BIN

A wooden bin of this design, insulated from heat and cold, will work in almost any situation. Keep in mind, however, that it will not be quite so easy to move, but on the plus side it works well outdoors all year round and doesn't require any additional insulation.

1 For the base, use a single board drilled with drainage holes. For the lid use thick wooden boards.

2 Make all four sides with a double skin of exterior grade plywood sandwiching 1 inch (2.5 cm) width insulation material.

3 Set up as for the plastic garbage can (see pages 102–103), but in this instance there is no need to add a layer of gravel.

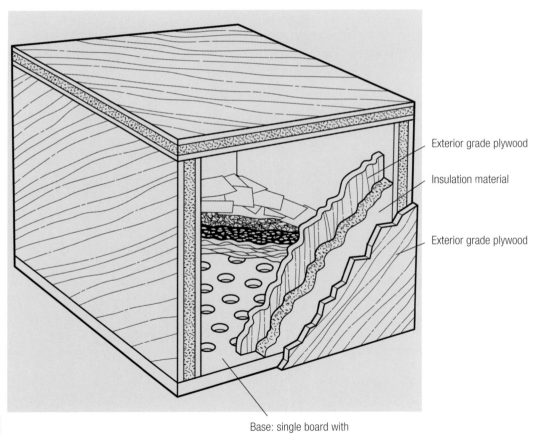

Exterior grade plywood

Insulation material

Exterior grade plywood

Base: single board with drainage holes

WHAT WORMS EAT

Most kitchen waste can be recycled through a worm bin, but a balanced mixture is best, rather than an excess of any one ingredient. Don't add too many citrus peels or onions, for example, as this can make conditions too acidic for the worms to work. Some garden waste, such as cut flowers, flower deadheads, young weeds and crop debris can also go into your worm bin, but exercise some caution since too much garden refuse could result in the bin heating up and upsetting the worms. Unlike garden compost, worm compost does not kill weed seeds or disease organisms.

Worm bins are also good for composting small amounts of cooked waste such as leftover rice and pasta. Meat, fish and dairy products are best avoided, as the worms take longer to

What can I put in my worm bin?

Do add

- Vegetable and fruit peels

- Leftover cooked potatoes and other vegetables

- Tea leaves and coffee grounds

- Crushed eggshells

- Cereals – rice, pasta etc

- A few annual weeds

- Kitchen paper, shredded paper

- Egg cartons, toilet roll centers

- Cut flowers, deadheads

Don't add

- Large amounts of citrus fruit or onion peelings

- Meat, fish, and dairy products

- Cat/dog feces

- Diseased plant material

- Plastic, glass, tin and other non-biodegradable items

- Large amounts of "greens" that could heat up

process these; they also tend to putrefy before the worms get to them and attract flies and rats. Fibrous materials such as shredded paper and cardboard are good to add to your worm bin, as these can help stop the compost from becoming too airless and wet. The worms will not break down non-biodegradable materials such as glass or plastic so don't put these in your bin.

Above Worms thrive on a relatively small but fairly frequent supply of fruit and vegetable scraps from the kitchen.

FEEDING THE WORMS

A worm bin works best if the worms are fed regular small amounts. This is particularly the case when you are just starting up a bin – once the worms are established and have started to breed, they will be able to process larger quantities of material.

Spread your kitchen waste (no more than 1¼ inches (3 cm) deep), over up to half of the surface area of your worm bin. Don't add thick layers – if the waste starts to heat up or putrefy, it will put the worms off. Once this layer of waste is well colonized by the worms, feed them again but in a different spot on that top layer.

Alternatively, you can bury the food just under the surface of the bedding or compost in small quantities, moving around the bin each time. Some people prefer this method because it keeps the worms and food out of sight, and it may deter fruit flies, but it does make it more difficult to monitor the progress of the worms. Keep the surface covered, with damp newspaper, for example, so that the worms are working right up to the top of the waste.

Top tips for healthy worms

- Don't over-feed, especially in winter.

- Add shredded paper and cardboard if the compost looks wet and soggy or begins to smell.

- Make sure excess liquid can drain away. It is useful, so use it in diluted form on plants and houseplants.

- Cover the food waste with layers of moist newspaper, cardboard or coir matting.

- Don't let your worm bin get too hot or too cold; a temperature of around 66°F (19°C) is ideal.

Left A thriving worm bin can process a considerable quantity of vegetable waste, but take care not to add more food than the worms can cope with.

HARVESTING THE WORM COMPOST

After you have been feeding your worm compost bin for several months, you should start to see dark, rich compost building up in the bottom of the bin. This nutrient-rich medium can be used to enrich the plants in your garden and pots.

To take out a small quantity of compost, simply scrape back the top layers of food waste with a trowel and take out what you need. Replace any worms you find in the compost back into the bin where they will continue to do their good work. Alternatively, you can wait until a larger quantity has accumulated and remove it all at once. This process will be slightly different depending on the type of worm composting bin you are using.

2 Once a third tray is nearly full of compost, the compost in the first tray should be relatively worm-free and can be removed for use (see top left photograph).

3 If there are any worms remaining in the compost you wish to harvest, simply pick them out and put them back into the top tray, or use one of the methods described below to separate them from the compost.

STACKING TIERED WORM BIN

A tiered worm bin makes it easy to harvest the finished worm compost.

1 When the first tray becomes full of compost, add a second empty tray and place the food in that. The worms will gradually migrate upwards to feed.

NON-STACKING WORM BIN

This type of bin requires a little more labor to extract the useful compost. Choose a dry, sunny day or use a light indoor space such as a hoop house. Scoop out the top 6 inches (15 cm) layer from the bin, where most of the undigested food and worms will be. Set it aside to put back into the worm bin once it has been emptied.

Empty out the rest of the compost onto a hard surface, plastic sheeting or tarpaulin. This will still contain some worms, but you can use the fact that worms move away from light (even on cloudy days) to separate them from the useful compost and reurn them to the worm composter. There are two methods:

Method 1 Spread out the compost in a 2 inch (5 cm) layer across your flat surface (see photograph above) and place a thick layer of wet newspaper over a third of the area. Leave for at least three hours. The worms will gradually move into the moister compost under the paper in their search for dark and damp conditions. Collect up the drying compost for use. Repeat the process until you have nearly all the worms in a small amount of moist compost. Scoop this up and put it back into the worm bin to start again.

Method 2 Divide the compost into little heaps, like molehills (see photograph above right). Leave for about an hour while

Above Worms migrate away from the light, so will congregate in the centers of your three small heaps (see method 2 below).

the worms move into the center of each pile. Scrape away the outer layers of the compost. Repeat at hourly intervals until all you are left with is small piles of compost teeming with worms. Put these back into your worm bin to start again.

Worm compost can be quite wet when first harvested, and will be easier to apply if you let it dry out slightly, but don't let it become dust-dry. If you are not using it right away, it can be stored in a bucket or bin for a few months.

Use the liquid from a worm bin right away if possible, as it may ferment if left and could explode sealed containers. See page 145 for how to use worm compost and the liquid feed.

8

OTHER COMPOSTING TECHNIQUES

Most compostable kitchen and garden waste can be processed through a traditional compost heap or worm bin. However, it may be preferable to use different techniques to recycle specific types of kitchen and garden "waste" such as autumn leaves, woody prunings and hedge clippings, food waste such as meat, dairy products and cooked food, and some perennial weeds. And then there is the ultimate in recycling, human feces, which should never be added to a general compost heap, but can be recycled through a compost toilet.

LEAF MOLD

USE FOR: ALL DECIDUOUS AUTUMN LEAVES

Autumn leaves from deciduous trees (not evergreens) rot down by the slow, cool action of fungi, rather than quicker-acting bacteria that are responsible for composting. Large quantities of autumn leaves would overwhelm a conventional compost heap; they are best recycled separately to make what is known as leaf mold. This is an excellent soil improver, lawn conditioner and potting mix ingredient. A small amount of dry leaves can be a useful source of "brown" material to balance the compost heap when you have an excess of "greens" such as grass clippings, for example.

HOW TO MAKE LEAF MOLD

1 Collect up fallen autumn leaves; all deciduous types of leaves can be mixed together.

2 Water the leaves if they are dry to help kick-start the decaying process. Collecting the leaves after a rainfall avoids having to do this yourself.

3 Stack the leaves where they won't blow away. There is no need to use a compost bin. You could pack the leaves into a black plastic sack, make a few holes in the bag with a fork and tie the top loosely. Store the sacks behind a shed, under a hedge or wherever you have space. Or fill a builder's bulk bag (the sort used to deliver sand).

4 You could also make a container by wrapping plastic or wire netting around a few stakes, then fill it with leaves. Let these sit for a year or two to decay before use.

Top tips

- If the leaves have fallen on a lawn, run a mower over them. If you leave the grass collection box off, the chopped leaves will be spread over the lawn, and will soon be taken down into the soil by earthworms.

- Alternatively, collect the chopped leaves and grass in the collection box and make them into leaf mold. The chopping and addition of grass clippings will speed up the decaying process.

Right Leaf mold is an excellent soil improver. It can also be used as a seed-growing medium.

MULCHING

USE FOR: GRASS CLIPPINGS; NEWSPAPER; CARDBOARD; AUTUMN LEAVES

Mulch is any material that is spread over the soil surface. Mulching can be a good way of recycling biodegradable waste, which will gradually be taken down into the soil by earthworms. Depending on the material used, a mulch may feed the soil, improve soil structure, help to keep the soil moist, and suppress weeds. Mulches are also good habitats for beetles, centipedes and other useful small pest-eating creatures.

A mulch is useful to the gardener when there are water shortages and dry summers – a good layer of mulch can help to retain the moisture that is in the soil by slowing the evaporation from the surface of the soil. As a consequence, plants don't need to be watered as much and summer watering bans don't necessarily mean dried-out gardens.

GRASS CLIPPINGS

1 Use your clippings in a layer up to 4 inches (10 cm) thick. Clippings release nitrogen as they decay so are best used around plants, such as leafy vegetables, which will benefit from a nitrogen boost.

2 Don't apply grass clippings right up to the stems of young plants. Leave a space around the base of the stems.

NEWSPAPERS AND CARDBOARD

1 Open out the newspaper and cardboard and spread over the ground, overlapping the edges for the best short-term weed control.

2 Top with grass clippings, straw or leaves to keep in place and hide unsightly appearance.

AUTUMN LEAVES

1 Spread moist, newly fallen leaves over the soil, in a layer of 1 inch (2-3 cm) thick. Do not use where bulbs have been planted as their shoots may have difficulty emerging through a compact layer of leaves.

2 In spring, rake back the leaves if you want to sow seeds.

116   *Organic Book of Compost*

Above Grass clippings can be used as a mulch, particularly around leafy vegetables..

STRAW AND HAY

1 Straw and hay supply some potash as they break down, so are good mulches for fruit bushes, woody-stem plants and trees.

2 Hay tends to contain weed seeds, which will germinate and grow, so keep this in mind when using it as a mulch in the fruit garden.

Top tips

- A mulch can absorb a lot of rain before it gets to the soil, so never apply a mulch to soil that is very dry.

- The reverse is also true – applying mulch to damp soil will allow the soil to retain its moisture, which can be a bonus in dry summers.

HIGH-FIBER HEAP

USE FOR: KITCHEN WASTE AND LOW-GRADE CARDBOARD AND PAPER

There can be times and situations when you don't have any garden waste, but would still like to compost kitchen and household waste. This tends to consist primarily of fruit and vegetable scraps and low-grade paper and card such as cereal boxes, egg cartons and toilet roll tubes.

A worm compost system is one option (see the chapter on worm composting, pages 92–111), but you can also compost these items in a conventional compost bin, making what is known as a "high-fiber" heap, a method developed by researchers at the Centre for Alternative Technology. The trick is to mix the soft wet kitchen wastes with crunched-up card and paper that act as "browns" and create the air spaces essential for the composting process to succeed. Don't crumple too tightly; an egg carton, for example, is ideal as it is.

1 Set up a compost bin on bare soil. Add a 12 inch (30 cm) or so layer of crumpled-up card and paper. If available add some worm-rich compost too.

2 Gradually fill the bin with a mixture of approximately equal volumes of kitchen scraps and crumpled card etc. It pays to start off slowly, giving the worms and other larger creatures that are the mainstay of this system time to move in and build up. Starting a high-fiber heap in late spring or summer as the weather is warming up is ideal.

3 Leave the lid of the bin ajar. This avoids any build-up of fruit flies. After a year or so, lift the bin off the heap. Remove finished compost, and replace the unfinished compost back in the bin so that it can continue to decompose.

GRASS-BOARDING

USE FOR: GRASS CLIPPINGS

This method was developed at the Centre for Alternative Technology for composting large volumes of grass clippings that would overwhelm the usual compost heap.

1 Layer the clippings with used paper towels that are an ideal "brown" to balance the "green" of the clippings.

2 If you do not have lots of used paper towels, then use corrugated cardboard and boxes – discarded packaging is available free of charge from some stores.

3 A bit of ripping and crumpling is needed, then add grass and cardboard to a compost bin, making sure that "greens" and "browns" are well intermixed. Where possible, remove packing tape from the cardboard before composting. Any remaining tape can be removed from the compost before use.

Below Grass clippings are a common compost ingredient and can also be grass-boarded. Take care never to use clippings from a lawn that has recently been treated with weedkiller.

BOKASHI SYSTEM

Uncooked fruit and vegetable waste is easily composted in a traditional compost heap or worm bin. Cooked food waste, however, does not compost nearly as well and may attract flies, rats, foxes and other vermin. Dairy products, fish and meat waste can cause the same problems.

BOKASHI TREATMENT

Originating in Japan, the Bokashi method is a "pre-treatment" for cooked and uncooked food waste, including meat, fish and dairy products. When Bokashi-treated food waste is added to a conventional compost heap, there should be no problem with smells or vermin. The treatment is also said to speed up the general composting process.

Bokashi is a fermentation process, carried out by micro-organisms that are added to the waste in a sealed bucket in the form of inoculated bran. Fermentation occurs in anaerobic (low oxygen/high carbon dioxide) conditions. Sugars are broken down into ethanol, lactic acid and carbon dioxide.

1 To start the process you will need two suitable buckets, each with a tight-fitting lid and a tap near the base to drain off excess liquid. It is easiest to use purpose-made Bokashi buckets, which can be purchased. You also need Bokashi bran, inoculated with the special mix of "Effective Microorganisms" (EM) required for the fermentation process. The process has little smell when working well, so you could keep the buckets in a kitchen or cool place in the house.

2 Food waste is added to one bucket in layers, with a sprinkling of bran over each layer. The waste is firmed down to exclude air as this is an anaerobic process. Any liquid produced is drained off every few days. Once full, the bucket is left undisturbed for two weeks – hence the need for the second bucket.

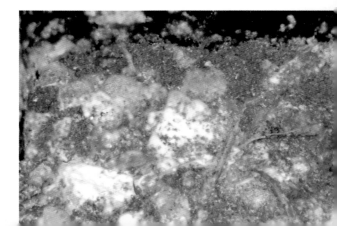

Right White mold on the surface of a Bokashi bucket is a sign that the process is working well.

Right Bokashi-treated material can be added to a traditional compost heap.

3 After two weeks, the material in the first bucket should have a white mold growing on it and have a sweet/sour vinegary smell. Empty the contents into an active compost bin, and start again. Alternatively you can empty the fermented kitchen waste into a hole in the ground or a compost trench.

If you have an active compost heap, it is best to put fresh fruit and vegetable scraps, and other food waste that would not attract vermin straight on to that heap, rather than taking up space in a Bokashi bin.

BOKASHI LIQUID FEED

The liquid that you drain off the Bokashi bucket contains nutrients from the food and is alive with beneficial microbes. The volume and composition of the liquid will depend on what you put into the container. Use it within a day or two of draining. It can be diluted and used as a liquid feed for container plants or watered on a compost heap. It can also be poured, undiluted, down kitchen and bathroom drains for a cleaner drainage system. The microoroganisms are particularly beneficial to a septic tank system.

What can be composted in this way?

The manufacturers claim that the following items are suitable for the Bokashi system:

- Plate scrapings and leftover cooked food of all sorts, including meat, fish and dairy, bread, pizzas, cake

- Vegetable peelings

- Meat and fish

- Meat and fish bones

- Dairy products

- Bread

- Tissues

- Coffee grounds

GREEN CONE

USE FOR: ALL HOUSEHOLD FOOD WASTE

The "Green Cone" is a particular brand of container that processes all household food waste – fruit and vegetable waste, but also raw and cooked meat and fish, dairy products and bones that are usually excluded from a traditional compost heap. It is not designed for garden waste.

This method is very useful if you want to reduce the amount of rubbish that goes into the bin collected by your local authority. Some authorities have reduced the frequency of rubbish collection to once every two weeks, which means that a bin containing food waste may begin to smell before it is removed. The cone is an effective way of reducing the volume of refuse you need to put out for collection and has the added benefit of providing nutrients for the shrubs and trees situated close to the cone.

Top tips

• If you see a blue/gray fur growing on the waste in your Green Cone, this indicates that the process is working.

• If you notice that there isn't much of this "fur" (particularly during colder weather) then add a handful of the accelerator powder that comes with the cone.

HOW TO USE A GREEN CONE

This container comes in two parts: a basket that is fitted below ground, with a lidded, green plastic cone-shaped structure above ground (see the photograph left). The design encourages aerobic decomposition in an environment that does not attract flies or other vermin.

It also differs from a compost heap in that the cone does not produce usable compost, and rarely, if ever, needs to be emptied. You can "harvest" the nutrients released by the decomposing food waste if you locate the cone near fruit trees or bushes, for example.

1 The cone should be sited in a sunny spot on soil with good drainage. Dig a hole large enough to sink the basket structure below the surface of the ground.

2 Fit the basket into the hole, and ensure that the top fits securely on to the basket.

3 Start to use your cone by putting any kitchen waste you want to recycle into the basket then cover with the top and leave it to decompose.

APPLE WORM HEAP

USE FOR: WINDFALL AND EXCESS APPLES

One drawback to having an apple tree in your garden can be dealing with windfalls and excess apples at the end of the season. Too many apples in a conventional compost heap will stop it from working properly, so this method may be a useful way to return those nutrients to the soil.

TO MAKE AN APPLE WORM HEAP

1 Start with a sturdy compost box; a heap of apples can be very heavy so plan accordingly. Put in a layer of apples, around 2 or 3 fruit layers deep, or more if apples are small.

2 Roughly chop the apples with a spade. This will help to speed the process and allow the worms to get to work quickly.

3 Cover the fruit with a layer of wet autumn leaves, old straw or rough compost. Repeat until you run out of apples, or the container is full, finishing with a covering layer of whatever material you have chosen.

4 Worms and other creatures will gradually move into the heap, making rich, moist compost. This can take as long as a couple of years. Note that apples can also be added to a compost trench (see pages 132–33).

Right Fallen apples are a wonderful source of food for birds and other wildlife in the autumn. Leave some for them to enjoy and turn the rest into compost.

PLANT SUPPORT STRUCTURES

USE FOR: WOODY BRANCHES AND STEMS

Although using extra woody branches and stems as supports for plants in your garden is not a composting method, it certainly qualifies as a method of recycling. Plant supports, can, of course, be bought at garden centers, but why not save yourself some money and contribute in a small way to saving the planet by making use of the excess materials from your own garden? Eventually these branches and twigs will begin to break down and decompose and can then be composted or shredded and returned to the soil (see below).

What you can make in the way of supports will depend on the size and strength of the branches and stems available. Freshly cut bamboo stems can be woven to make a trellis, 6-10 feet
(2-3 meters) long branches and stems can be used to make a wigwam for runner beans, squashes or sweet peas to climb and twiggy prunings are good as pea supports. You can also make use of these in herbaceous borders.

WILDLIFE HEAP

USE FOR: WOODY BRANCHES AND STEMS

Sometimes the woody material generated by your gardening is not useful for supports, and you might not want to make it into mulch. You can recycle these bits and pieces into a valuable habitat for garden creatures instead!

1 Heap the woody material in an out-of-the-way corner of the garden. Compact the heap as much as possible – trample it down if necessary – and fill gaps with rough compost, leaves, clumps of grass and soil etc.

2 The heap can take many years to decay completely, but will provide food and shelter for many creatures – from hedgehogs and frogs, to beetles and centipedes – in the meantime.

Right Cut branches make excellent supports for these white-flowered runner beans and a great way to recycle long branches.

SHREDDING AND CHIPPINGS

USE FOR: SHREDDED WOODY BRANCHES AND STEMS

Another method for disposing of woody branches and stems from your garden is to put them through a shredder. You can buy a shredder, but it is also possible to rent fairly high-powered ones that will make short work of substantial amounts of woody material (see page 56).

MAKING SHREDDING AND CHIPPING COMPOST

1 Put branches and twigs through the shredder following the manufacturers" advice on operating the machinery. You can use conifer prunings as well as those from deciduous trees.

2 The shreddings can then either be added to a mixed compost heap or if you have large quantities of shreddings, made into a separate compost heap.

Top tips

- Shreddings and chippings can be used to mulch informal paths, especially those in the garden, without prior composting.

- Living wood (still green under the bark) is much easier to shred than dead wood and it will compost much more quickly.

3 Mix with grass clippings or other "greens" and water if dry. Watering with a nitrogen-rich liquid such as nettle or comfrey liquid can help the process along.

4 Within a few months the material can be used as a mulch around shrubs and other established plants, or gradually added to a mixed compost heap.

Left Comfrey or nettles can be used to make a liquid that can help a shredding and chipping compost heap get to work.

NASTY WEED HEAP AND WEED BAG

USE FOR: PERENNIAL AND PERNICIOUS WEEDS

Perennial weeds such as crabgrass, celandine, bindweed, lambsquarters, chickweed, dandelions and Japanese knotweed (see box, opposite page) can regrow from roots, stems or other plant parts (depending on the weed). Some of these plant parts may be killed in the composting process; others may not and could grow again when you spread the compost.

Burning this type of weed is not recommended; the roots and stems will have taken up valuable minerals from the soil, often from areas where other garden plants do not reach, so burning them wastes valuable resources and the smoke pollutes the atmosphere.

In most cases it shouldn't matter if a few weeds grow again from compost spread on your garden, but if you are trying to get rid of a particularly difficult weed such as bindweed or celandine, try the weed bag or the "nasty weed" heap.

USING THE NASTY WEED HEAP METHOD

When clearing an overgrown garden or allotment plot you may have large quantities of perennial weeds that can be put into a separate weed heap.

1 You can simply put them into a solid-sided compost bin, adding "greens" if necessary, and leave them to compost for as long as it takes. Cover tightly.

2 Alternatively, make a heap on the ground on a sheet of black plastic and cover completely with more black plastic to prevent any growth escaping. New shoots are likely to appear from the roots under the plastic at first, but they will then die off.

3 Leave the heap for as long as it takes for all signs of plant life to disappear completely. This may take a couple of years to accomplish.
Using the weed bag method

Left These weeds are well on their way to becoming compost in a nasty weed heap.

USING THE WEED BAG METHOD

The weed bag method kills perennial weed plants so that they can then be added safely to a more conventional compost heap without the risk of regrowth.

1 Take a strong black plastic bag (old potting compost bags turned inside out are good for this) and fill it with the weeds. If they are mostly roots and stems, add some "greens" such as grass clippings or weed tops to the bag.

2 Tie the top of the bag and store it somewhere out of the way for six months or more. A sunny spot will speed up the process but is not essential.

3 When you open the bag again you should find a black sludge, which can be added to a compost heap. Any bits that are not fully rotted can be put back into the bag and set aside to continue to decompose fully.

Japanese knotweed

Japanese knotweed (*Fallopia japonica*) is one perennial weed that should be treated with extreme caution. It is one of the most invasive weeds, spreading in the wild and displacing natural vegetation. It is a bad idea to cause it to grow in the wild. All parts of the plant and any soil contaminated with it must be disposed of with due care.

You can compost the cut stems, if they are first dried out completely to a dark-brown color. They must be dried on a surface that does not allow them to root into the ground. Roots and crowns (the base of the stem) must be disposed of in some other way. Contact local experts for advice; do not just put it into a green waste bin. For more information on this and other invasive weeds, check the Resources list on pages 186–187.

TRENCH COMPOSTING

USE FOR: UNCOOKED FRUIT AND VEGETABLE WASTE

Fruit and vegetable waste from kitchen and garden, including windfall apples and all Bokashi-treated food waste (see pages 120–121), can be composted simply in a "compost trench" in the garden. This method is usually used over the winter and early spring; crops are then grown in that spot in the following summer, making use of the food and moisture released by the decaying waste. This method is not suitable on heavy, poorly drained soils.

A compost trench is a good way of recycling stems and leaves from winter brassica crops (broccoli, cabbage, Brussels sprouts). It has the added benefit of burying and killing mealy aphids and whitefly, two pests commonly found on old brassica plants.

Runner beans are traditionally grown on a compost trench, while French beans, zucchini, pumpkins and squashes also enjoy the moist, rich conditions.

MAKING A COMPOST TRENCH

1 Mark out the area you want to use as a trench with string and stakes on either end. Dig a trench about the width and depth of your spade –about 12 inches (30 cm) wide and 12 inches (30 cm) deep – and 6-8 feet (2 meters) long (see photograph opposite, top left). Heap the soil up along the edge of the trench.

2 Starting from one end, add suitable waste to the trench as material becomes available (see photograph opposite, top right).

3 Cover each addition of material to the trench with some of the soil that you have dug out (see photograph opposite, bottom left). Repeat this process each time you add material to the trench.

4 When the trench is full, cover it completely with the remains of the soil (see photograph opposite, bottom right). This will probably make a mound, but this will gradually settle over the next couple of months. You can then use the site for planting beans, zucchini and other vegetables.

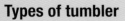

Types of tumbler

There are lots of different models of compost tumbler, but there are three basic types of tumbling mechanism:

- Cranking handle – this requires the least effort (see photograph top left).

- Physically spinning the container on an axle (see photograph bottom left).

- Rotating the tumblers on a molded plastic base or rolling it around the garden (see photograph top right).

- Some models are easier to turn than others, so it pays to try and find one to test out (when it is full, not empty) to ensure that you can turn it easily.

TUMBLER COMPOSTING

A compost tumbler is a compost bin that can be turned (or "tumbled") to mix and aerate the contents. This is equivalent to turning a compost heap (see page 57), without removing the compost from the bin. Regular turning speeds up the rate of composting, with some tumblers claiming to make compost in as little as three weeks. A compost tumbler is a self-contained unit, which does not need to be in contact with bare soil. For this reason it is less likely to be troubled by vermin.

A tumbler does need to sit on a level surface, however, and for some types you will need a tray to collect any liquid that drains from it.

USING A TUMBLER

1 The normal rules of composting (a good mix of greens and browns, adequate water etc) apply to composting in a tumbler. In general, tumblers are designed for batch composting, and need to be filled at one go, or over a period of a few days at most. You will need to store material produced between batches, or have a tumbler as just one part of your composting system.

2 If you have used a good mixture of ingredients and have chopped up larger items, a tumbler may produce compost in as little as 21 days, though not all tumblers make this claim. If the compost is not ready to use when you empty the tumbler, store it in a compost bin to finish off.

Left It may look as though aliens have landed, but in fact these are all compost tumblers.

METHOD: COMPOST TOILETS

USE FOR: HUMAN FECES AND URINE

Perhaps not the method for everyone, but the greatest of our wasted resources is human feces and urine since vast potential sources of plant foods are flushed down the toilet every day. If you really get interested in waste recycling you might consider installing a composting toilet in your garden. Check local rules and legislation governing the use of composted human waste.

Non-flush toilets have been in use around the world for thousands of years and range from a simple hole in the ground where the feces and urine dissipate into the soil around, to more sophisticated elevated toilet blocks, where the feces are composted and the resulting "humanure" is harvested and used as you would use other compost.

You can build your own compost toilet or install a purpose-built one. For more information about composting toilets check out the Resources list on pages 186–187.

9

HOW TO USE
YOUR COMPOST

Recycling kitchen and garden
waste at home to produce
compost and other soil
improvers is satisfying in itself,
but the real benefits come when
you use the end products in the
garden. Whatever size your plot
or pot, and whatever you grow,
these are valuable resources.

WHAT DOES COMPOST DO?

Compost and other recycled garden materials are known as "bulky organic materials." They feed the millions of tiny soil-living creatures that are responsible for creating the soil structure. Bulky organic materials improve and protect soil structure, helping light soils to hold moisture and heavy soils to drain more easily. Composts also supply plant foods as they decompose in the soil. Plants grown in composted soil are more resistant to pest and disease attack.

Below Many of the benefits of using compost are invisible to the naked eye. Compost helps to create a diverse, active community of creatures living in the soil. They manage the soil so that our plants can thrive.

USING COMPOST

WHEN IS IT READY?

Compost is ready to use when it is dark brown and soil-like, and has a pleasant earthy smell. It does not matter if it isn't just like the fine "multi-purpose" compost that you buy in bags for sowing and potting. Even if it is a bit lumpy and stringy, and there are twigs and eggshells still visible, you can use it as it is, or sieve it to make a finer product.

However, unless you are using a compost tumbler or have turned the heap several times, the compost won't be ready all at once. Some material at the top of the bin will be only partly decomposed when there is "finished" compost at the bottom.

To get the best from your finished compost, use it within a few months. It is much more valuable when it is on the garden, rather than taking up space in your compost bin!

All garden compost can be put to good use – on vegetables, fruit and ornamental plants, and on lawns and containers too. It can be an ingredient in homemade potting mixes. It is a good source of potassium and trace elements and gives a reasonable supply of phosphate.

Above You will find the compost that is ready to use at the bottom of the heap.

WHEN TO APPLY

Compost is best applied in spring and early summer when plants are growing and can take up the nutrients. Don't apply compost in late summer as this can encourage soft, sappy growth that may not harden properly in time for the winter, leading to winter injury. As compost is quite stable and is slow to break down in cold weather, you can also apply it later in the year with little risk of nutrients being washed out.

HOW MUCH COMPOST

There is no need to be precise in the quantities you use. Concentrate on soils and plants that need feeding, but don't overdo it. As a rough guide, use no more than one 12 gallon (50 liter) wheelbarrow load for every 16 square feet (5 square meters) of growing area per year, about ½ inch (1 cm) deep.

Left Spread compost on the surface of the soil, or fork it into the top 6 inches (15 cm) of soil.

Right Roses thrive on a mulch of compost every year or two.

WHERE SHOULD IT GO?

The best use for garden compost will depend on how rough or fine it is and whether it contains viable weed seeds.

Rough compost

Rough compost that still contains woody bits, eggshells, fruit pits and other material that has not fully decomposed, is best applied as a mulch around fruit trees and bushes, roses and other shrubby plants. Earthworms and other soil-dwelling creatures will gradually incorporate it into the soil.

Some nutrients will be released from the compost during the first growing season, but plants will still be getting some benefit from it a year or two after application. Alternatively, you can sift rough compost and use it as you would finer compost (see below).

"Weedy" compost

If your compost tends to produce a flush of weed seedlings when spread on the soil, it will cause less work if you incorporate it into the soil – for example, when you are planting fruit trees or bushes, or potatoes on the vegetable plot. Fork it into the top 6-8 inches (15-20 cm) of soil, no deeper. Alternatively apply the compost in a situation where you can easily hoe off any weed seedlings that appear.

Fine crumbly compost

Compost that is reasonably free from lumps, twigs and weed seeds can be used in any of the ways already mentioned, and others too.

Fork or hoe it in to the soil (no deeper than 6-8 inches (15-20 cm) as this is where most of the plant's feeding roots are) or spread it on the surface for the worms to take under. It can also be used to feed and improve a lawn (see pages 152–153) or mixed with other ingredients to fill large pots, windowboxes and troughs.

Sifted compost

Compost can be sifted to give a very fine product, which is ideal if you want to use it in potting mixes or for top-dressing plants in pots. Many of the fibrous bits and lumps in the compost will break up in the sifting process; others can be returned to the compost heap or used as a mulch around trees and shrubs. A simple garden sieve is cheap to buy or you can improvise – for example, by attaching a piece of wire mesh (about ⅖ inch (10 mm) grid size) to a wooden frame.

To make it easier on your back, try fitting the sieve into the top of a large plastic tub. Rocking the tub back and forth is less hard work than holding a sieve full of heavy compost. If you are producing large amounts of compost, you might want to invest in a rotary sieve.

USING WORM COMPOST

WHEN IS IT READY?

Worm compost is ready to use when it is dark and crumbly, and you can't recognize any of the original items that went into it. Because of the way it is made, worm compost tends to be available in smaller quantities than traditional compost.

WHERE SHOULD IT GO?

As worm compost is made primarily from kitchen waste, it usually has a good texture and is free of weed seeds. It is usually richer than garden compost, particularly in readily available nitrogen. For these reasons, worm compost is ideal for use in homemade potting mixes, particularly those for greedy feeders such as tomatoes and squashes. Add it to purchased potting composts as an additional source of plant foods and to hold moisture. You can also use it for top-dressing plants in pots. Worm compost can be used in the garden in a similar way to traditional compost. Apply it in spring and summer to plants that need to put on vigorous growth.

The liquid drained from a worm bin is also rich in plant nutrients. Dilute it in a ratio of 1 to 10 and use as a liquid feed for pot- and container-grown plants, or water it onto the garden compost heap to recycle the nutrients.

Left Generally you don't need to sieve compost, but it is worthwhile if you are making potting mixes or top-dressing plants in containers.

USING AUTUMN LEAVES AND LEAF MOLD

These materials have slightly different uses to conventional composts. Leaf mold is low in readily available plant nutrients, so it can be used at any time of year and in larger quantities than compost. It is excellent for protecting and improving the soil structure and is a useful ingredient in homemade sowing and potting mixes. It is also a good autumn top-dressing for lawns

Newly fallen leaves

Newly fallen leaves can be spread over bare soil to protect it over winter. Rake the leaves back before sowing into the soil in the following spring.

Young leaf mold

Leaf mold can be used on the garden as soon as the leaves begin to break up and crumble easily in your hand. This will take about a year, though more resistant species, such as oak or chestnut, may have to be left longer. Spread it as a mulch or incorporate it into the top 6-8 inches (15-20 cm) of soil almost anywhere in the garden. It is particularly valuable as a soil improver for crops such as carrots and annual flowers that don't like lots of nutrients. In this case, spread a thin layer of a half inch (a few centimeters) over the soil surface (the autumn before sowing if possible), and hoe it in lightly before sowing any seeds into it.

Well-rotted leaf mold

After another year or so, you will have what is called "well-rotted" leaf mold. This is dark brown and crumbly, with no real trace of original leaves. This product can be used as above, but it is also valuable in seed and potting composts. You can sift it if necessary.

Comfrey leaf compost

Comfrey leaf compost is a nutrient-rich potting mix that contains levels of available nitrogen and potassium in proportions particularly suitable for growing tomato plants. It can also be diluted with extra leaf mold for raising other young plants.

To make comfrey leaf compost, mix well-rotted leaf mold with chopped fresh comfrey leaves in equal proportions by volume. Put the mixture into a plastic lidded bucket or garbage can and leave for a few months or over winter until the comfrey has completely decomposed.

Right To make a nutrient-rich potting medium known as comfrey leaf compost, mix equal volumes of comfrey leaves (shown right) and leaf mold. Leave to rot for several months.

USING COMPOSTED WOODCHIPS AND SHREDDINGS

Above Woodchips will gradually rot down when used in a pathway.

Left Woodchips make a nice informal path surface in gardens.

Woodchips and shredded woody prunings are very slow to break down and do not immediately provide nutrients or improve the soil structure in the same way as compost. Even after they have been composted separately for a year or more (see chapter on other methods of composting, pages 112–137), they will still be decomposing. Don't dig them into the soil as they can use up nitrogen that could otherwise be feeding your plants (this is known as nitrogen robbery).

However, they can be useful as a mulch around established trees and shrubs to keep down weeds and retain moisture, and will very gradually add organic matter to the soil. Spread them in a layer 2-4 inches (5-10 cm) thick, starting about 4 inches (10 cm) out from the trunk. You can do this at any time of year provided that the ground is not frozen and that you make sure the soil is thoroughly moist first.

Woodchips and shreddings can also be used, fresh or composted, to mulch informal paths. Dig out the pathway to a depth of 6 inches (15 cm) or so, line with a permeable weed-proof membrane if weeds are likely to grow up from below, then cover with woodchips. After a year or so, you can dig out the partially rotted woodchips for use on the garden, replacing them with a fresh batch.

Above If you only have minimal supplies of compost, put it to best use in your vegetable plot to provide nutrients for your crops.

COMPOST USE IN SPECIFIC SITUATIONS

Below are a number of suggestions for the use of various types of compost in a variety of gardening situations.

VEGETABLE PLOT

Hungry plants such as potatoes and members of the brassica (cabbage) family make the best use of compost or worm compost. Apply before sowing or planting in spring and early summer.

Winter brassicas such as Brussels sprouts and sprouting broccoli can benefit from a second application in July or August. On poorer soils, vegetables such as squash, Swiss chard, onions, beans and beets will also benefit from the application of compost.

If you use crop rotation in your planting scheme, carrots, peas and parsnips will generally thrive on leftover nutrients from a previously fed crop. Use leaf mold where these crops are to grow to improve the structure and water-holding capabilities of poorer soils.

FRUIT TREES AND BUSHES

Before planting, add compost and/or leaf mold to the planting area, and mix it in to the top 6-8 inches (15-20 cm) or so of soil. Use both leaf mold and compost on poor soils and leaf mold alone where soil is already nutrient-rich.

Raspberries: these greedy-feeders benefit from an annual mulch of compost in spring each year, unless the soil is already very rich.

Gooseberries, hybrid berries: generally a compost mulch every other year is quite enough; use an annual application if growth is poor.

Strawberries: apply compost to plants in early spring before growth begins if growth was poor the previous year.

Fruit trees: for the first two years after planting apply a 3 inch (7-8 cm) mulch of compost in March to help provide a good supply of nutrients during the growing season and to conserve soil moisture. Trees on dwarfing and semi-dwarfing rootstocks may still need a compost mulch every year or two. Where the soil is already nutrient-rich and the trees growing well, use leaf mold instead.

Above Berries and other soft fruits thrive on a diet of compost.

LAWNS

In spring, apply fine compost when the grass starts to grow. The compost will supply nutrients, improve the soil texture (which helps moisture retention and drainage) and help any "thatch" (dead grass on the surface) to decompose.

Apply leaf mold in the autumn to improve soil structure. Spread the compost or leaf mold in a layer about a quarter inch (1 cm) thick and sweep it into the turf with a stiff garden broom. Time this just before rain if you can, so the material is washed down to the soil surface. Mixing it with coarse sand can make it easier to spread and is beneficial on heavy soil.

ORNAMENTALS

Roses: Mulch with compost every year or two, depending on the soil fertility, using a leaf mold mulch in alternate years.

Herbaceous plants: mulch with compost every two or three years.

POTS AND CONTAINERS

Perennial fruit, herbs and ornamental plants grown in containers long term: Feed with sifted traditional or worm compost,

Left, top and bottom Spread a thin layer of compost on your lawn then sweep it into the turf with a garden broom.

preferably in spring when they start to make leafy growth. Scrape off any moss or weeds and the top inch (2-3 cm) of the existing growing medium and replace it with fresh compost.

Above Sweetpeas require rich soil in order to thrive and will benefit from a generous mulch of compost.

Spring-planted hanging baskets and containers of annual flowers or vegetables:

Top off baskets and containers with compost later on in the growing season to give them an additional boost.

MAKING YOUR OWN SEED AND POTTING MIXES

SEED SOWING MIXES

Try using sifted well-rotted leaf mold on its own or mix it with up to 25 percent coarse sand or perlite to improve drainage. Seed sowing mixes do not need lots of nutrients, in fact high nutrient levels can inhibit germination of small seeds.

POTTING MIXES

On its own, compost is too rich for most plants and does not have the right structure for use in pots. However, it is valuable if mixed with other ingredients. Try combining equal proportions of compost, loam and leaf mold, or use 3 parts leaf mold to 1 part worm compost. Coarse sand or perlite can be added for extra drainage and organic fertilizers for a richer mixture. Experiment with your own mixes until you find one that suits your needs.

Above Measure out the appropriate volume of each ingredient for your potting mixture.

Above Mix all the ingredients together. Do this two or three times to make sure they are thoroughly mixed. Water if necessary.

Above Use your nutrient-rich potting mixture to give your plants the best start possible.

10

THE CREATURES IN YOUR COMPOST HEAP

A compost heap isn't just a heap of dead stuff; it is a hotbed of biological activity. One pinch of compost can be home to literally millions of microscopic creatures. In technical terms, a compost heap is a complex food web, comprising a whole range of creatures that rely on each other for survival, often as a source of food. They appear, like magic, just when they are needed.

WHO LIVES IN THE BIN?

Many of the species that live in your bin or heap actively contribute to the composting process, while others, such as ground beetles and centipedes, will use it as a temporary refuge as they hunt for a meal. They in turn attract useful predators to the garden such as birds and frogs. Amphibians (frogs and toads) love compost heaps as they are damp and full of food; they will help to keep the snail and slug population in check.

So you can see that a compost heap is a bit like a mini-beast nature reserve. In addition to producing compost, which helps your garden grow, a compost heap can be a reservoir of beneficial creatures that help control garden pests. A compost heap can provide temporary shelter for small animals such as lizards and mice, which in turn eat slugs and snails, common pests in many gardens.

NO PESTICIDES PLEASE

If you are new to composting, the first sight of all these tiny creatures in your compost heap might have you reaching for the insecticide spray. This is, of course, the last thing you should do; kill the creatures and there would be no compost.

Below This Common earwig, found in compost heaps, is an excellent mother, protecting her eggs from predators.

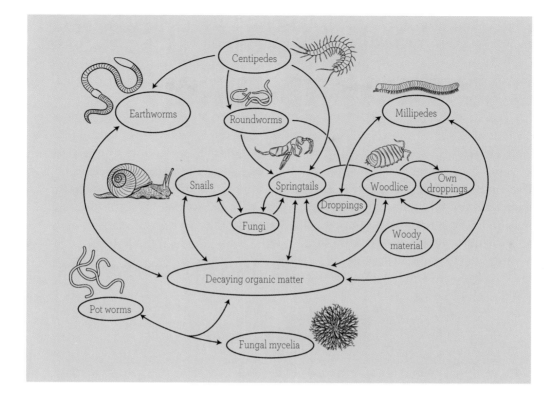

WHO EATS WHOM?

Decomposition is part of the natural world. Many of the species you encounter have been around recycling organic matter for millions of years.

The bulk of the decomposition work is carried out by micro-organisms – the bacteria, fungi and actinomycetes (bacteria that grow filaments). Then the smaller invertebrates such as the roundworms, mites, springtails and worms move in to break the waste down and digest and process it further. Woodlice, beetles and millipedes will start to appear along with their predators, the centipedes and spiders, until there is a whole food web working together to produce compost! The food web above illustrates which organisms eat what within the compost bin. If you follow the arrows from the decaying organic matter you will be able to see which organisms feed off other organisms by either eating droppings or eating other organisms within the compost bin, helping to keep a balance in the population.

LEVEL ONE DECOMPOSERS – BACTERIA AND FUNGI

BACTERIA

These microscopic organisms are the most important members of the compost food web. Bacteria digest the plant material by producing the appropriate enzyme to digest whatever material they find themselves on. It is their ability to produce a variety of enzymes that gives them the edge over other micro-organisms.

When you put organic waste into your compost heap it will already have some bacteria on its surface. As the bacteria digest the organic material, they start to break it down into its basic elements and, at the same time, they multiply at an incredible rate. The metabolic heat of these micro-organisms is what produces the initial heat in a compost heap. The speed at which they work is illustrated in the heat that can build up in a heap of grass clippings if you leave them undisturbed for a few hours.

There are many kinds of specialized bacteria working in different temperature ranges. Psychrophillic bacteria –which work best at around 55-60°F (13-15°C)– get to work on organic waste straight away. If you notice your heap working in the winter, these are the bacteria that are at work. Increasing temperatures produced by psychrophillic bacteria allow the next group of bacteria, the mesophillic bacteria –that work best at temperatures 70-90°F (21-32°C)– to get to work. Along with the next group, the thermophillic bacteria, they can produce temperatures of 160°F (70°C) and above in industrial-scale composting sites.

FUNGI AND ACTINOMYCETES

Once the bacteria have done their work, the fungi and actinomycetes move in and the decaying process is on its way. The actinomycetes give the compost a very pleasant earthy smell and can often be mistaken for mold as they form grayish, cobwebby growths. Fungi get involved during the final stages of composting, when the organic material has been changed to a more digestible form. Most fungi live in the outer layer of compost on the surface.

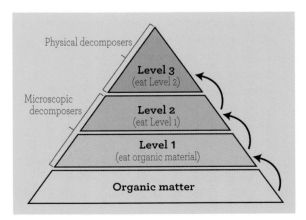

LEVELS TWO AND THREE DECOMPOSERS

Once the bacteria have done the initial chemical break down of the tough cell walls of the material in the compost bin, larger organisms move in to help transform the organic waste matter by physical action such as chewing, sucking and grinding. Below are some of the most common invertebrates you may find in your compost heap.

ANIMALS WITH NO LEGS

Nematodes

Nematodes (roundworms) are very small, so you are unlikely to see them! They include bacteria, fungal spores, slugs and beetles in their diet. Although you may have come across nematodes as plant pests, those found in the compost heap will not damage plants and are an important link in the compost heap food web.

Enchytraeids

Also known as pot worms, Enchytraeids are thread-like white worms less than 2 inches (1-60 mm) in length. These are harmless, but can be an indication of acidic conditions, which is why they are commonly seen in clumps of kitchen waste and in large numbers in a worm compost bin that is not working properly due to acid conditions.

Brandling worms

The worms you will see in a maturing compost heap are brandling worms (*Eisenia foetida*), which are the ones used in a worm compost system (see page 97). They are "detritivores," feeding primarily on partly decomposed plant material, sucking up the waste that has started to be broken down by the bacteria. They produce a highly fertile worm manure, called worm casts or compost. The common earthworm (*Lumbricus terrestris*) lives in the soil rather than a compost heap. It plays a vital role taking compost down into the soil and mixing it in.

Slugs and snails

Slugs and snails have a bad reputation for eating living plants, but they are also part of nature's rubbish disposal system and play a useful part in the composting process. Some species of slug prefer to feed on decaying vegetation. Unlike some of the other invertebrates in the compost, slugs can secrete cellulose-digesting enzymes to help break down the food they eat and are therefore not reliant on bacteria to carry out this digestion for them. So like them or loathe them, some slugs are very handy to have in your compost bin.

ANIMALS WITH SIX LEGS

Ants

If you do not disturb your compost heap for a while, you may find that it has been colonized by ants. Ants feed on seeds, other insects and fungi, all of which a compost heap will provide. Ants can benefit a compost heap by bringing fungi and other organisms into their nests, increasing the biodiversity in the heap. They tunnel through the contents of the heap, creating air pockets and enriching the compost by moving minerals from one place to another. It is easy to assume that if you get rid of the compost heap, you will get rid of the ants in your garden – but these creatures are so ubiquitous in gardens that one nest more or less makes very little difference. Never be tempted to add an ant killer to a compost heap. If you want to discourage them, keep the contents of the compost bin moist, and turn it more regularly.

Springtails

Springtails are very common in compost heaps, feeding on fungi, pollen, decaying matter and some roundworms. Look closely and you will see them running in and around tiny particles in the compost. You may also see them hopping and flicking themselves into the air. They do this with a "spring"-like structure underneath their belly that catapults them into the air. They are the compost bin "cleansers" as they also eat up droppings from other small creatures, meticulously cleaning themselves afterwards.

Bristletails

Bristletails feed on algae and decaying organic matter. The two-tailed species in particular is common in compost heaps.

Earwigs

Earwigs can be easily identified by their forceps-like pincers, which they use for defence. Most earwigs feed on decaying plant matter but some species are predatory and feed on a variety of other insects. Many species are wingless and live in the soil or in enclosed spaces. Predatory earwigs will enter plant stems to hunt for stem-boring larvae. They hide during daytime, becoming active at night.

Beetles

Beetles are invaluable! You may come across many types of beetle in your compost, including rove beetle, ground beetle and feather-winged beetle. The feather-winged beetle feeds on fungal spores; its young feed on decaying vegetables. Adult rove and ground beetles prey on snails, slugs and vine weevil larvae, keeping their numbers down.

Flies (mainly true flies with two wings)

Flies play an important role during the early stages of the composting process, helping to transport bacteria to the contents of your compost heap. The tiny fruit fly (*Drosophila*) is the most common fly seen in compost heaps. These tiny flies have a rather bulbous-shaped lower body, which is frequently orange or light brown in color. They are relatively slow flyers, often hovering around fruit, even indoors.

Above Ground beetles are one of many types of beetle found in the compost heap and garden – they eat slugs and vine weevil larvae among other pests.

Below Common earwigs are also a feature of compost bins but are mostly active at night.

Above This impressive-looking Pseudoscorpion is only a few millimetres in length.

Fungus gnats

Fungus gnats are attracted to moisture and fungi, so are common in compost bins. These gnats are also members of the fly family, but tiny (about 1 mm) in size. They can be recognized by their all-black, rather skinny bodies, compared to that of fruit flies, and their gnat-like manner of flying. They can sometimes be observed crawling on the bedding in a worm composter.

ANIMALS WITH EIGHT LEGS

Spiders

Not all spiders are web makers; some hunt their prey. Spiders feed on insects and other small invertebrates, helping to keep the insect population in balance. The most common spiders found in compost heaps are the woodlice spider (*Dysdera crocata*), the garden spider (*Araneus diadematus*) and sometimes the common house spider (*Tegenaria*), although the house spider will not tolerate damp, cold conditions.

Daddy longlegs

You may sometimes see a daddy longlegs in your compost heap. They are easily mistaken for spiders, with their eight long legs and carnivorous habits. But the similarities end there. Daddy longlegs don't spin webs and they don't produce venom. If you look at the main body at the center of all those dangly legs you'll notice that it's all one piece. Spiders have two parts to their bodies – a cephalothorax (head and thorax) and the abdomen. In daddy longlegs these two parts are fused together.

False scorpions

False scorpions or Pseudoscorpions are small arachnids –rarely more than 1/10 inch (3-4 mm) long –, related to the true scorpions, spiders and mites. They resemble scorpions in having relatively large pincers for catching prey, but they lack the stinging tail of true scorpions and are completely harmless. They are usually various shades of yellow and brown. Little is known of their mode of life, but most species live outside under stones, under loose tree bark, and in leaf litter, moss and other debris, including in your compost heap.

All species are carnivorous and probably feed on various tiny insects, worms and other small invertebrates. They generally walk fairly slowly, waving their pincers in front, but all can run swiftly backwards or sideways without turning, in a crab-like manner, if disturbed or threatened.

One interesting fact about the false scorpion is that they have a remarkable habit of seizing hold of the legs of flies and hitching a ride with the flies while they are in flight! In this way false scorpions can move into compost heaps and other suitable locations.

Mites

Mites are a very mixed group of arachnids and are extremely numerous in the compost heap. They are also found at all levels of the compost food web (see page 159). Typically they are small and globular with short legs.

There are hundreds of different species of mites living in every conceivable habitat. Some are predators; others eat organic decaying matter while some others eat fungi and bacteria. Other mites will eat nematodes, slug eggs, springtails and insect larvae.

ANIMALS WITH MORE THAN EIGHT LEGS

Millipedes

Millipedes are long and cylindrical, with two pairs of legs per body segment. They feed mainly on decaying plant tissue but will eat insect carcasses and excrement. They perform many functions, such as soil turnover, aeration, conversion of nitrogen and phosphorus and incorporation of organic matter into the soil.

Centipedes

Centipedes have flattened bodies and a single pair of legs per body segment. They are fast-moving predators and found mostly in the top 2 inches (5-6 cm) of the compost heap. They prey upon spiders, mites, insect larvae, slugs and woodlice.

Right Millipedes perform a number of functions in the compost heap, making them invaluable creatures to have in your bin.

Woodlice

Also known as sowbugs and pill bugs, woodlice bugs curl up into a ball when they feel threatened, whereas a sowbug remains flat. Woodlice are not insects but isopods, a common type of arthropod. They are commonly found in soil and under decaying organic matter such as wood or leaves, and under pots and boxes in sheds and greenhouses. If left exposed to the air, they will die within a few days.

Woodlice break down cellulose fibers in woody material and other rotting vegetation, making it more accessible for other creatures in the compost food web (see page 159). If you find large numbers of woodlice in your compost heap, this may indicate that it is too dry and that you need to add water and/or to mix in more "green" materials.

EXPLORING YOUR COMPOST HEAP

Now that you have become familiar with some of the creatures that live and work in your compost heap, the next time you visit you may want to take a little time to stop and admire them.

You can usually spot the larger creatures, such as woodlice, worms and centipedes, moving around on the surface of the compost heap as soon as you lift the lid to the compost bin. If you dig a little deeper into semi-decomposed compost, a whole new world of bugs will be opened up to you. All you need to be able to see most of them is a magnifying glass, a shallow plate or a glass jar, and a bug identification card or book (see Resources, pages 186–187). Place a small sample of almost ready compost on the plate and take a look; you'll be amazed at how alive it is!

There are many insect observation chambers available now; these allow you to collect your bugs and study them without them running away! Once you have finished, remember to put them back into the compost heap.

If you want to take an even closer look you could invest in a pocket microscope with up to x40 magnification. Such a microscope will allow you to get close up and see the really tiny bugs, such as the small mites and springtails.

Top left The Common shiny woodlouse breaks down cellulose fibers.

Bottom left Centipedes are fast-moving creatures within the compost community.

11 COMPOSTING IN THE COMMUNITY

Compost-making isn't just an activity done by individuals at home; it is being done on a huge scale in purpose-built centralized sites. Compost is also being made in schools as part of the learning day, by community groups and in community gardens. This chapter gives a short introduction to these various activities and also introduces Master Composters, volunteers from all walks of life who promote and support composting in all parts of the community.

WHAT HAPPENS TO THE COMPOSTABLE WASTE WE THROW AWAY?

Increasingly, households are required to separate the waste they throw away. One category for separation is garden waste that you could compost at home, which is then taken to a large-scale centralized composting site. This is a great step forward from all our waste going to landfill, but it would be a retrograde step if it discouraged people from composting at home, which is by far the most energy-efficient way of dealing with green waste. However, even if you are a keen composter, it can be useful to have somewhere else to dispose of items such as thorny bramble and rose prunings, for example. Green waste that is taken to household recycling centers is also processed in the same way.

Centralized composting is carried out on commercial composting sites and on farms where the farmer has diversified into composting waste and using the end product on his or her own land.

The volumes of waste treated are huge. Material is usually heaped into long piles (known as windrows) and turned frequently by machinery. Temperatures easily reach 140-160°F (60-70°C), and ready compost can be produced in three months or less. The whole process is carefully monitored to make sure that the end product does not contain contaminants, including plant and animal diseases.

Green waste treated this way produces a compost which tends to be low in readily available nitrogen, but with good levels of potassium (potash) and reasonable levels of phosphorus. Some composting sites sell the compost – loose or in bags. Depending on the grade, it can be a coarse mulch or a finer compost.

Left Green waste composting being done in a small windrow.

Food waste is another separation" category that is collected in some areas. Again this is composted at centralized sites, but because of varying degrees of legislation depending on where you live, the process becomes more complicated. Under some rulings, food waste has to be composted in enclosed containers, known as "in-vessel systems." This keeps out birds, rodents and other vermin, thus avoiding the potential spread of disease. The composting process here is the same as at an open-air site with windrows, but it is more thoroughly managed and monitored.

Above Kitchen waste from large institutions, such as schools and hospitals, can be composted in centralized locations.

COMPOSTING WITH
THE COMMUNITY

Just because you don't have space at home or have access to a collection made by your local public works, doesn't mean that you can't get involved in making compost. There are all sorts of community composting schemes running in many different places. Many are run by involvement from the local community, but the projects vary widely in scale, the way they are run, and what they do.

A community-composting project may work with its local council to provide curbside collection services for green waste. The project may compost garden waste on a relatively small scale, with a voluntary workforce and very little technical input. A county scheme may compost garden waste in its group of villages, asking people to deliver the material; other schemes have an organized system for collection of the waste, which is then composted

Above Many communities run composting schemes, varying in scale.

away from the village or town. Yet other schemes are composting garden and food waste on a larger scale in an in-vessel composting system.

The benefits of community composting go beyond the environmental ones of reducing waste going to landfill, reducing peat use and improving soil structure. Community composting projects can, amongst other things, also help provide training, raise awareness of waste and community issues, provide employment, and contribute to a local area's social cohesion.

LEARNING WITH COMPOST

Over the last decade or so, gardening, and food growing in particular, has been reintroduced to schools. Garden Organic has been one of the leaders in this revolution with its Garden Organic for Schools and its involvement in the Food For Life Partnership.

The gardening methods used in schools are usually organic, which means that compost-making (and using) is something that many children now learn about and participate in at school.

The benefits of composting in schools go far beyond soil improvement. It brings together teachers, pupils, grounds maintenance and catering staff to work cohesively. Compost-making can be used as a learning aid in many areas of the school curriculum, and it reduces waste and the cost of dealing with waste.

A school can easily deal with gardening green waste, fruit peelings and teacher's lounge coffee grounds and teabags using the home composting methods. To deal with food waste (including cooked food) from the kitchens, some schools are using small-scale "in-vessel" composters. The food waste is composted in a fully enclosed container, so a more diverse range of materials, including cooked food leftovers, dairy, fish, meat and small bones, can be safely and effectively composted. These small-scale in-vessel composters can be turned like a compost tumbler, which mixes and aerates the contents, so the process is hotter and quicker than a conventional compost heap.

They range in size –3-6 feet (1-2 meters) long– and capacity, but all can be filled a little at a time, in keeping with the needs of the catering staff.

As with all composting, "brown" material is needed to balance the "green" catering waste. Wood chips or sawdust are usually recommended for this. Although wood pellets can be purchased, the most cost-effective source would be sawdust from a local sawmill or carpenter's shop (as long as the wood has not been treated with a preservative), or woodchips from a tree contractor.

Below Food waste is put into one end of this "in-vessel" composter. Turning the handle moves the waste through the vessel, so it emerges as compost at the other end.

Getting as many staff and pupils involved as possible is very important to foster a sense of ownership and community. If all pupils and staff have some understanding of the composting process and why the school is making compost, fewer mistakes are likely to be made. Pupils and staff will also make an effort to compost waste as they understand why it is important for the school and environment. Compost-making can easily be introduced to the whole school through assemblies and lessons on sustainability and the environment. Posters make striking visual aids to act as prompts for pupils around the school. The messages of sustainable living and reducing waste do not stop at the school gate. Schools are ideally placed to make a positive impact on educating the community.

A tried and tested system for getting pupil participation is to have "Compost Monitors." This is a model developed by Garden Organic, where a group of nominated pupils is responsible for the daily collection of compostable materials from around the school. The size of school and age of pupils will affect how this system works in practice. It is advisable for the school to invest in a number of kitchen bins to collect the compostable waste. These can be placed in the teacher's lounge, lunch rooms, break areas and wherever fresh food waste is generated.

The big advantage of this system is that once it is up and running, the staff responsible can take a less active lead, allowing the pupils to take over the day-to-day tasks and in doing so learn many valuable lessons.

MASTER COMPOSTERS

Once you've got the composting bug you are quite likely to enjoy enthusing about the magic of compost to your friends, neighbours and family. Some people take this a step further and become "Master Composters" – volunteers who work in an official capacity, helping to increase composting in their local community by spreading the word, and offering advice and support to people who want to compost more effectively.

Garden Organic is a leader in the UK promoting and teaching the skills of home composting among many audiences including individuals, communities, schools and professionals. In partnership with local authorities and waste service providers, we deliver the Master Composter Programme, which over the past 20 years has involved recruiting, training and supporting thousands of proactive volunteers who have taken their learning and skills out into their communities to further promote the message. Garden Organic's training includes information on all scales of composting (as discussed in this book), the basics of how to compost at a home level, and how to go about promoting the compost message to your community. They are then supported for at least a year through advice, provision of materials to use for displays and information in the form of a manual and regular updates.

The fact that Master Composter volunteers come from every age group and a wide variety of backgrounds is one of the strengths of this scheme. Master Composters can reach areas that other compost promoting activities cannot reach – they talk to their friends, family and neighbors in a language that they can understand. They may write articles for their community newsletter, attend village fairs and it has even been known for a Master Composter to hold a compost-themed children's birthday party!

Master Composters really make a difference in changing people's attitudes and behavior and they are an essential part of national strategies to increase environmental awareness and to reduce the amount of waste that just gets put in the garbage can.

So whatever way you want to get composting – at home, in the town or at school – get going and, like the Master Composters, pass it on!

12 FREQUENTLY ASKED QUESTIONS

Although composting requires a relatively easy set of skills and principles to learn, questions invariably arise about the various methods and problems. This section tries to provide answers to a number of questions that most commonly seem to trouble those new to composting.

MAKING COMPOST

How can I keep composting my kitchen waste over winter when the weather is cold?

A well-insulated worm compost bin or one kept in a relatively warm location is ideal for winter kitchen waste composting. The worms will work more slowly, but should still keep going (see pages 92–111). A compost trench is another alternative (see page 132).

My compost bin smells awful. What have I done wrong?

You have probably put too much kitchen waste or other "greens" into the bin without sufficient "browns" to soak up moisture and create air spaces. This means that the composting process has turned anaerobic and it is putrefying rather than composting.

The remedy is to empty the bin and refill it, adding more "browns" to the mix. If you can't bring yourself to do this, just leave the bin alone for a month or two and it may improve on its own.

How can a compost heap get so hot?

As plant material is broken down, the energy that went into making it is released in the form of heat. The heat build-up is a result of the oxidation of organic substances and the manufacture of carbon dioxide and water. As molecular bonds are broken and reformed, energy is released. Temperatures in the middle of a commercial heap can reach 175°F (80°C)!

Should I buy an activator to use on my compost heap?

Purchased activators usually supply nitrogen or microbes, both of which will be present in a compost heap anyway. You can make compost very satisfactorily without an additional activator if you follow the advice in this book.

I've seen slugs and snails in my compost bin. Will making compost just increase the slug problem in my garden?

Not really. Slugs and snails are part of the natural composting process. The compost heap provides them with an ideal habitat so they have no particular reason to leave. They may be eaten by beetles, centipede or roundworms in the compost bin or just die of old age! Slug and snail eggs also have many predators. Some slugs, such as the leopard slug (*Limax maximus*), only eat rotting organic matter and will not harm living plants.

Why do I get lots of tiny little flies in my compost bin?

These are fruit flies, which lay their eggs on fruit skins and peels. They are particularly common in warm weather, around a compost bin that has a lot of kitchen waste in it.

To reduce the problem, keep a lid on your kitchen bin; empty it regularly and use a good mix of material in your compost bin; bury kitchen waste under a layer of other compost or some shredded paper when you add it to the bin rather than leaving it on the surface. Leaving the compost bin lid ajar prevents the numbers building up.

How long does it take to make compost?

This depends on which method you use. If you are "cool-composting" it will take around 12–18 months to make compost that is ready to use. If you are "hot-composting" then you will probably get some compost after six months. This does depend on what raw materials you've added, the location of the compost bin and the time of year the heap was started.

The only garden waste I have is grass clippings and it just goes into a slimy mess. What should I do?

To make compost you need approximately equal amounts of greens and browns. There will be no air in a heap of grass clippings, hence the slimy mess. You have a number of options; grass boarding (see page 119), leaving the grass clippings on the lawn or using them as a mulch (see pages 116–117).

I'm using an old plastic garbage can as a compost bin. Why does my compost smell of rotten eggs?

The most likely cause is lack of drainage. A build-up of liquid will make the heap airless, so it rots rather than composts. It is probably best to cut the bottom off the garbage can so excess liquid can easily drain away.

Old-fashioned gardening books talk about carbon to nitrogen ratios with regard to compost-making. What does this mean and is it important?

A carbon to nitrogen ratio (C:N) simply describes the proportion of carbon to nitrogen in a given material. These days we tend to talk about "greens" and "browns" instead. Greens have a very low C:N ratio; browns have a high C:N ratio.

The optimum for making good compost is around 25:1, but it is a lot simpler for the home composter to aim for equal proportions of green and brown material. We encourage people to experiment to find the balance that works best for them.

Some typical C:N ratios

- Kitchen waste   15:1

- Grass clippings   19:1

- Chicken manure   10:1

- Horse manure   25:1

- Leaves   40:1

- Straw   80:1

- Paper   170:1

- Fresh sawdust   500:1

Can I compost diseased plants?

Plants infected with soil-borne diseases such as white rot on onions, brown rots on fruits, wilts of tomatoes and cucurbits, and clubroot on brassicas are best not added to a compost heap. These types of disease can survive for many years in the soil and are unlikely to be killed in a compost heap. Many other common diseases, such as mildew, only survive on living plant material, so infected plants can safely be composted. (See also "What can I compost" section, pages 60–77.)

Can I compost plants that have pests on them?

Pests that only live on living plant material will not survive a compost heap. Pests that live on dead and decaying plant material or have a resistant stage are more likely to survive. A compost trench (see page 132) is a good way of dealing with pest-infested material.

Can I compost poisonous plants?

Yes. The toxins will not harm the creatures that make compost or plants on which you use the compost. Take care if you are shredding any poisonous plants. Always shred outdoors and wear a dust mask.

A HOME FOR YOUR COMPOST

Do I need more than one compost bin?

You can make compost with just one bin, but there are advantages to having two or three. You can start a new heap while the older one is maturing. In a large garden or if you make a lot of compost, you may choose to have several bins dotted around the site.

I don't have a sunny spot to locate my compost bin in – does it matter?

No it doesn't matter; it just means the composting process may be a bit slower if the bin is in a shady spot.

Where is the best place to put my compost bin?

Put the bin where it is easy to get to all year round. If you put it in an inconvenient spot, you are much less likely to use it.

Should I drill air holes in my plastic compost bin?

There is no need to do this. Getting air into the bin is much more dependent on the structure and mix of materials in the bin than having air holes.

Do I have to put my compost bin on bare soil? Will concrete do?

You can make compost in a bin on a hard surface. The composting creatures will still find their way there. Start the heap off with a thick layer of newspaper or cardboard to soak up any liquid produced by the decomposing material in the bin.

WORM COMPOSTING

What happens if I remove worms along with the worm compost by mistake?

Don't worry if there are a few worms left in the compost you are using. They will move on to a suitable place.

What happens if the worm bin freezes?

If there was a fair amount of compost in the bin, you may find that the worms have clustered together in the center and will still be alive. They will start into activity when the temperature rises. If the worms do freeze, there should still be worm cocoons in the compost that will hatch out when the weather warms up.

How much waste will the worms process?

A very rough estimate is around 1 pound (500 g) every 4–5 days in summer, less in winter. It will vary with the surface area of the bin, the number of worms and the temperature.

Can I put grass clippings in my worm composter?

You could add small amounts as long as they are mixed with an equal volume of crumpled paper or cardboard – but as they are usually available in large quantities, grass clippings are best composted in a traditional heap.

Will the worms try and escape from the bin?

If conditions are right, the worms will be happy to stay in the bin. If you find them around the lid, trying to get out, this is an indication that something is wrong. Check that they have not been swamped by food (so that it is heating up or putrefying) and that the bedding and compost are not waterlogged.

My worm bin has started to smell and the food waste isn't being processed. What should I do?

Overfeeding and/or too much moisture are likely reasons for this. Check that the bin is draining properly. If you can still see live worms, stop adding waste, and mix in moisture-absorbing materials such as scrunched-up paper towels, egg cartons and cardboard. Add a sprinkling of crushed eggshells to make conditions less acid. If you cannot see any live worms, you may have to clear out the bin and start again.

There are lots of tiny flies in my worm bin – what can I do?

These are fruit flies – they are harmless but annoying. Empty your kitchen bin daily, bury the waste when you add it, and keep the surface well covered with damp newspaper to reduce the problem. If you keep the lid of the bin ajar they will not fly up in clouds when you lift the lid.

My worm compost contains lots of thin white worms – are they harmful?

These are probably enchytraeid worms (also called pot worms), which process waste. They are harmless but their presence may indicate that the compost is getting too wet or acidic. Check the drainage and add some crushed eggshells.

What do baby worms look like?

Baby worms are simply smaller versions of the adults. If you look carefully you may see tiny lemon-shaped "cocoons" in the compost. Each of these contains up to eight tiny developing worms. They can survive conditions that would kill the worms (e.g. freezing conditions).

What happens when I go on holiday?

You don't need to worry. Worms in an established bin can survive for at least three weeks without any food, and even after that the population will only decline slowly. Don't be tempted to add extra amounts of waste to the bin before you go – it will only start to putrefy.

Can I remove compost from the bin at any time?

Small amounts of compost or full trays from a tiered worm composter can be removed at any time. If you keep an ordinary non-stacking worm bin outside, however, spring and summer are the best times to empty it. The worms will then have enough time to build up more compost before winter sets in and can retreat into it in cold weather.

THE CREATURES IN YOUR COMPOST BIN

I think rats may have been visiting my compost bin. Is the compost still safe to use?

Yes, the compost is quite safe to use. You could take the added precaution of wearing gloves when handling it.

I'm worried that if I make compost it will attract rats. Is this true?

If rats visit your compost heap they will already have been living in the vicinity, you just won't have been aware of them. They are more likely to be attracted if you put cooked food waste in the bin, and if you put it in an out-of-the-way spot where it is rarely disturbed. The number of compost heaps has increased markedly over the last few years, but there has not been an increase in reports of rats in gardens.

Ants have taken over my compost heap and are spreading around my garden. How can I stop them?

Ants are just one of the range of creatures that help make compost, although if they are present in large numbers it can be a sign that your heap is too dry. They may establish a nest in your compost bin. However, this is not a particular problem, and is not the reason why you have them all around your garden.

If you wish to encourage the ants to leave your compost bin, turn the compost and mix in plenty of "greens" in the form of grass clippings, vegetable and fruit peelings if the heap is still actively working. Watering the heap to keep the mixture moist will also help to deter them.

HEALTH AND SAFETY

Are there any health and safety aspects I should consider when making and using compost? I am fit and healthy.

If you are in good health, the only precautions you need to take when making and using compost are the normal good hygiene measures that you would take when gardening:

- Cover any cuts and grazes with a waterproof bandage

- Keep your tetanus vaccination up to date

- Wash your hands thoroughly after handling compost

- Do not include non-vegetarian pet feces in your compost-making.

I have heard stories about people getting ill from composting. Is it really safe?

The few cases that have occurred where people have become ill after making or using compost generally relate to those who have a poor or compromised immune system, and those who are allergic to fungal and other spores.

The particular area of concern is the inhalation of "bioaerosols" – fungal spores, micro-organisms and other tiny particles that are released into the air when you turn a compost heap or empty a bin. To reduce the release of bioaerosols, keep the contents of your compost bin moist, and avoid turning or otherwise disturbing the heap. If you have a poor or a compromised immune system, then always wear a dust mask when spreading the compost.

RESOURCES

Garden Organic

www.gardenorganic.org.uk

Garden Organic is the UK's leading organic gardening charity. Dedicated to promoting organic gardening in homes, communities and schools, we use innovation and inspiration to get more people growing in the most sustainable way possible.

Formerly the Henry Doubleday Research Association, Garden Organic has been at the forefront of the organic movement for over 60 years. Based at Ryton Organic Gardens just outside Coventry (UK), the charity continues to get people growing through hands-on projects including Master Composters and Masters Gardeners. The charity is also the home of the world-renowned Heritage Seed Library – a collection of around 800 heritage vegetable varieties not found anywhere else in the world.

Garden Organic welcomes members from across the world, who support our charitable work, and in return members have access to a wealth of organic growing information and advice.

Garden Organic Home Composting and Master Composters

www.gardenorganic.org.uk

We have a wealth of composting information within the composting pages. To find out more about our Master Composter Program and other community volunteering programs, please visit the Projects section of our website.

The Organic Gardening Catalog

www.organiccatalog.com

The catalog for organic and environmentally friendly gardeners – compost bins and tumblers, worms bins, organic seeds for vegetables, heritage and modern varieties, herbs, flowers and green manures, organic composts and fertilizers, biological pest controls, organic gardening books and gifts. All purchases help to fund the work of Garden Organic.

Organics Recycling Group

www.organics-recycling.org.uk

The objective of the group is to promote the sustainable management of biodegradable resources, covering both aerobic and anaerobic technologies.

Brooklyn Botanic Garden

www.bbg.org/gardening/compost_education

Compost enthusiasts and advocates have the opportunity each spring to take the Master Composter Certificate Course with the NYC Compost Project hosted by Brooklyn Botanic Garden.

Centre for Alternative Technology (CAT)

www.cat.org.uk

CAT's visitor center has interactive displays on composting and other sustainability issues, a free information service and courses on a range of topics.

Bio-based and Biodegradable Industries Association

www.bbia.org.uk

BBIA is the UK trade body for companies producing bio-based and biodegradable products and promotes the circular bioeconomy.

Compost Education Centre

Compost.bc.ca

A nonprofit organization providing composting and ecological gardening education.

Composting Council Research and Education Foundation

Compostfoundation.org

Supports initiatives that enhance the stature and practices of the composting industry by supporting scientific research, increasing awareness, and educating practitioners and the public to advance environmentally and economically sustainable organics recycling.

Compost Now

Compostnow.org

Farmers, artists, technologists, social workers, musicians, poets, community activists, mothers and fathers working together to reimagine food waste management and rebuild our depleted soils.

Cornell University

http://compost.css.cornell.edu

Maintained by the Cornell Waste Management Institute (USA), the website provides access to a variety of composting educational materials and programs developed at Cornell University.

DEFRA

Department of Environment, Food and Rural Affairs

www.defra.gov.uk

The government department that deals with food and its production, plus much of the legislation relating to compost and waste. Website also includes further information regarding the disposal of pernicious weeds.

Local government websites

Your local government website may include information on buying compost bins and collection caddies. They may also advertise composting events and sources of advice in your area.

Minibeasts – an identification guide

by Peter Smithers. Illustrated and published by John Walters

www.johnwalters.co.uk

An illustrated key to help you name all of the common types of mini-beast that you encounter on a bug hunt through your compost bin and garden.

Recycle Now

www.recyclenow.com

Includes information on all sorts of waste, with activities for primary and secondary schools on recycling and sustainability.

For information specifically on home composting, and availability of compost bins at a subsidized rate from your local council see: www.recyclenow.com/home_composting

The Field Studies Council

www.field-studies-council.org

Resources and courses on offer. Particularly interesting in relation to the creatures in your compost bin chapter.

INDEX

Page numbers in italics refer to illustrations/captions

Picture credits

Ray Spence: pages 2, 8, 9, 14, 17, 18, 22, 24, 25, 26, 27, 30, 33, 34, 35, 38, 40, 41, 42, 43, 44, 45, 46, 47, 48, 49, 51, 53, 54, 56, 57, 58, 59, 60, 63, 68, 76, 78, 81, 83, 92, 94, 95, 96, 107, 115, 121, 122, 125, 127, 133, 134, 141, 142, 144, 147, 148, 150, 152, 154, 155, 156, 175, 176, back cover

Garden Organic: 10, 11, 12, 21, 80, 90, 91, 97, 99, 102, 110, 111, 119, 120, 140, 143, 149, 170, 171, 173

John Walters: 158, 162, 163, 164, 165, 166

Francesca Foley: 7, 16, 117, 129, 138, 153, 168, 172

Pauline Pears: 130, 131, 137, 151

Alamy: 108, 111

Shutterstock: front cover (top, Zocchi Roberto; middle, Lightspring; bottom, Jesse David Falls; arrows, Fancy Tapis); 2-3 (Wstockstudio); 4 (HollyHarry); 5 (mexrix)

ACKNOWLEDGEMENTS

This book was written by a team of experts from Garden Organic, the UK charity for organic gardening.

Harriet Kopinska PhD

Harriet has five compost bins, two open heaps, one leaf mold bin and a worm composter. Harriet worked as Home Composting Coordinator for Garden Organic for a number of years and has such in-depth knowledge of all aspects of composting that her specialist subject on "Mastermind" could definitely be compost!

Jane Griffiths MA

While working at Garden Organic, Jane was involved in all aspects of the Master Composter program. She has a degree in Geography and has spent over a decade wording with volunteers in a number of areas.

Heather Jackson BSc (Hons)

Heather has a keen interest in the natural world and in particular a passion for plants and composting. She worked as a Project Coordinator at Garden Organic where, as part of the Sustainable Waste Management Team, she researched everything to do with compost and worked with the Master Composter volunteers throughout the country.

Pauline Pears MSc

Pauline worked for Garden Organic since the days when organic gardening was a fringe activity. She worked with Lawrence D. Hills, one of the "fathers" of the organic movement and the founder of charity Garden Organic. Pauline ran Garden Organic's horticultural advisory service and, although retiring from the charity, remains technical editor of its membership magazine. She has written many organic gardening books and edited the *Encyclopaedia of Organic Gardening*. She still finds compost making exciting and usually has six or so heaps going at once.

We would like to thank many people for their inspiration and enthusiastic sharing of knowledge, including: all Master Composters and Master Composter Coordinators; Dr Margi Lennartsson, formerly the Head of Programs at Garden Organic, for passing on all her years of composting knowledge; Pete Smithers from Plymouth University, for continued enthusiasm for spiders and bugs; John Walters for supplying fantastic photos of all types of mini-beasts; David Hawkyard for help on worm composters; Jamie Blanchfield for drawing an inspirational diagram and for lots of input in the initial stages of the book; Gary Marsland, Tony Curtis and Mary Buckley for proof-reading and helping with the text over the year; Geoff Borin for the elegant design; Steve Dew for the informative line illustrations throughout; Ray Spence and Francesca Foley for photographs; Dr Anton Rosenfeld, David Garrett and Sarah Brown for bringing this publication up to date for the latest edition; and finally thanks to our four authors for the continued cups of tea, cake and reassurance during the many months of writing, editing and proofreading.